EXPLORE THE MEANING OF
LIFE, TIME AND CREATION

YOUR ORIGIN AND DESTINY

IVAN RUDOLPH

Copyright © 2020 by Ivan Rudolph

All rights reserved. No part of this book may be reproduced or transmitted in any form or by any means, electronic or mechanical, including photocopying, recording, or by any information storage and retrieval system without the written permission of the author, except where permitted by law.

This book is a work of non-fiction. Unless otherwise noted, the author and the publisher make no explicit guarantees as to the accuracy of the information contained in this book and in some cases, names of people and places have been altered to protect their privacy. The views expressed in this book are those of the author alone and not of the publisher or anyone else.

Scripture quotations, unless otherwise stated, are taken from The Holy Bible, New International Version® NIV®.Copyright ©1973, 1978, 1984, 2011 by Biblica, Inc. Used by permission. All rights reserved worldwide. New International Version® and NIV® are registered trademarks of Biblica, Inc. Use of either trademark for the offering of goods or services requires the prior written consent of Biblica US, Inc.

Co-published by Bublish, Mount Pleasant, South Carolina and author Ivan Rudolph.

Copies of this book may be ordered from all major online retailers.

Paperback: 978-1-64704-046-8
Hardcover: 978-1-64704-047-5
eBook: 978-1-64704-048-2

Library of Congress Control Number: 2020902807

DEDICATION

This book is dedicated to all those committed Scientists, of whatever faith or none, who have improved our life, health and lifestyles.

We are indebted to you. Thank you!

It is also dedicated to those Christians who have modelled the Christian life of love, faith and service in a selfish and often hostile world that denies them free speech.

We are indebted to you. Thank you!

ENDORSEMENTS

"This book contains one of the most logical explanations of man's purpose in the Universe that I have ever read! It is beautiful. It thrilled me.

Ivan deals with the issues for which humankind has struggled to find answers for so long—Creation, Heaven, Time, future events and life after death (including NDEs), with accurate and sharp precision. And he provides us with sound, logical biblical answers.

—**Rev. Dave Smethurst, International Evangelist with a highly effective and loving ministry, and founder of a number of orphanages in Eastern Europe**

"Your Origin and Destiny provides a well constructed pathway to understanding the deeper meaning of life. This book is a compelling testament to the reality of God, creation and the reason we are here.

Being the only survivor of a fatal airplane crash and experiencing life-after-death, I was fascinated by Ivan's ability to address life and eternity in a way that adjusts the focus of the reader. After personally having a life-altering revelation and experience of Heaven, it is rare to find someone who is able to effectively articulate the relation between this life and the next in a way that provides clarity and logic.

This book provides generous answers to the student searching for the meaning of life, as well as offers compelling argument to change the mind of the intellectual who believes God is a crutch for the weak. I recommend this book to anyone searching for meaning in life and to those who want to know more about the reality of a Divine Creator.

—**Capt. Dale Black, Prominent Airline Pilot and Trainer, Founder of Dale Black Ministries**
Author of two excellent books,
Flight To Heaven* and *Visiting Heaven

"As a church Minister, I encounter death and the dying often, and experience a wide range of ideas, reactions, emotions, questions, and postulating about death. Ivan Rudolph's proposition of 'shadow theory' and the 'transfer principle' in harmony with a careful study of the Bible, combine into a useful framework for all who will cope with or support those facing what eventually comes to us all—dying.

The Bible makes it clear we are made to transcend earthly time, to eventually greet our own eternity—this book provides a thoughtful discussion about the relationship between our short earthly sojourn and God's eternal purposes, for every one of us. Science keeps faith honest, and faith is strengthened as serious scientific research digs deeper and deeper into our human understanding of the gift of life."

—**Mark Taylor, Minister at Stoke Row Chapel, Oxfordshire, England**

"As an avowed protagonist of "Old-Earth Creation", I was pleased to see that Ivan's very interesting and, to me, ***quite original take on time*** fitted in perfectly with this—as easily as the instantaneous elimination of the bulldog bite as attested to by Doctor OB Bowker in 1975. This was a miracle, essentially very rapid creativity, chronicled by Ivan in this book.

To me the section on the supposed spontaneous creation of life as opposed to it having been brought about by God was most interesting. I have long struggled with the probability of the former occurring. Ivan mentions that his and my Professor in the Geology Department of the University College of Rhodesia, Professor Geoffrey Bond, felt the same way in the mid-1960s.

I feel sure that many will find themselves closer to God after reading this book."

—Ian "Sandy" Sanderson, Maths HOD
and Physics Teacher in the UK

"I have read Ivan Rudolph's manuscript with great interest and the subjects he tackles capture my attention as they are the kind of things which I have meditated on for many years.

I am especially interested in his insights about Time. Also, having been with people as they passed on, I have witnessed some truly extraordinary events as they approached death, and I am comforted by his research on Near Death Experiences.

This, together with accounts given to me by people who have themselves been at or near death, convince me that his comments verify much of what I have seen and believe. I think the book will be of great interest and comfort to others."

—Roland Pletts, international Christian author,
Minister and speaker

"This book is incredibly thought-provoking, whilst providing a thoroughly well researched analysis of such important fundamental concepts. The focus clarifies the concept of ***Time*** in the scriptures—and how translations have muddied the waters.

Using a "teacher's" clear and easily understood style we learn the different stages of God's work: Creation planned first in Heaven, and Creation then actioned on earth, as well as Creation which takes place over time and encompasses a Theory of Evolution. We learn a great deal about God's creativity and love—past, present and future—and our role in his family."

—Julie Tennett, Critic and Editor

"I love the book! It is so easy to read and is honest. I find your first-person rendition includes me as a reader. I find your honesty in examining various views engaging and non-threatening. This makes me as a reader feel safe. I have read reasonably widely on the topics you cover; however, nowhere have I met such honesty of discussion, which is disarming. Herein lies its strength.

Yours is the most lucid explanation of Creation that I have encountered yet. I have shared this with several Christians who enjoy searching out a matter.

It sheds light on a complex reality. I pray that many minds will be enlightened and lives changed for God's glory. Thank you for writing it.

Your explanation of Time rings true with me."

—**Rev. Ian Feeney, founding Principal of Xavier School (today's Citipointe Christian College in Brisbane Australia), former Official of the Queensland State Department, School Chaplain, and a Christian Counsellor**

CONTENTS

Preface 11
Introduction 17

Part 1—Were You Created? Or Did You Evolve? Or Both? 23

    1—Questioning Evolution 25
    2—The Inspired Answer 33
    3—Pondering One Miracle of Healing 38

Part 2—Time on Earth and Time in Heaven 47

    4—Glimmerings of Time 49
    5—Digging Deeper into Time and Prophecy 60
    6—Time in Heaven 68

Part 3—Your Time In the Afterlife 77

    7—NDEs, Shadow Theory, and Transfer Principle 79
    8—Two-Stage Theory and God's Creativity 95

Part 4—Our Time Begins 101

    9—The Words of Creation 103
    10—Genesis Unlocked: Key Words of Creation 117
    11—The Days of Creation (Genesis 1:1 to 2:3) 129

Part 5—Your God—And You 141

    12—Origins (Genesis 2:4 onwards) 143
    13—God Speaks Creatively 151
    14—Qualities of God 163

Part 6—Your Personal Destiny 179

    15—God In Our Afterlife Experiences 181
    16—God's Family 195
    17—Destiny 209

Acknowledgements 219
Endnotes 221

PREFACE

Science without religion is lame; religion without Science is blind.

—A truism stated by Albert Einstein[1]

A childhood question we never quite found the answer to in the playground, in school, or at home was "Who am I?" Later it likely became lost in the noise of life without ever being answered fully. Nowadays, with numbers of fine Scientists and leaders in industry and technology becoming increasingly alarmed by developments in artificial intelligence (AI), the question starts to puzzle and challenge us again, "Who **really** am I? How fundamentally superior am I to a sophisticated robot?" Robots can already invent their own private language and share information with other robots. They express awareness, logic, feelings, and independence.

It may shock us, but Science does not actually know the answer to man's superiority, nor to the essence of Time, Consciousness, Energy or Love, vital though these are to our existence. Check them out on the internet "what is Energy *really*?" and so on. For example—we know a huge amount how one form of energy converts into another, and how to measure it, how it travels and other characteristics, but what it truly is eludes us. The same is true for Consciousness and Time. In addition, we experience and value Love without being able to pinpoint it either. Our Universe runs with elegant Physics and Chemistry laws, but mankind is ignorant of their origin. We are babes in the woods of existence, whatever existence is.

Conceptually, humanity is in trouble. Can these mysteries be solved in time for us to face some of our greatest challenges ever that loom ahead?

This book can and should help.

However, projected developments in cyborgs, who are part person part machine, make us uncertain even as to what humankind is. Adam Clark Estes writes in Gizmodo Oct 2013:

> **"The dream of the cyborg is coming true at an exhilarating rate. As humans get better and better at making machines, we keep attaching those machines to our bodies to make ourselves better humans. It seems at times that the only question left is if we can put a human brain in a robotic frame.** *Actually, it's not a matter of "if". It's a matter of when."*

Similarly, Elon Musk 2017 believes we have reached a crossroads in our evolutionary history—we either evolve with the machines we have created and become one with them, or we face extinction as a species. Could Elon be right?

Within these pages, I will attempt to explain why it is that our best and brightest Scientists and philosophers do not at present know what Time, Consciousness and so on are. My motivation for tackling these mysteries is to guide readers into a fresh and valid understanding of them, and to explain carefully why these answers have not been given previously.

This book searches out who we genuinely are—our origins, the purpose and significance of our lives on Earth today, and the destiny that lies ahead for us.

I will introduce God as the ultimate Consciousness who originally made (created) everything with a deep purpose, one which is worth our careful examination because it involves ourselves.

God's creativity is a central theme that runs through the Bible from the first pages to the last: from the initial Genesis narrative to the stunning Revelation descriptions of an upcoming New Creation comprising New Heavens and a New Earth.

This is thereby a Creation-centred book, and I start where I began myself with questions regarding Creation and Evolution while at university studying Geology. It is the first question we have to resolve once and for all—are we simply the product of energy cooling into particles after the Big Bang and then slowly assembling under mysterious laws of Physics and Chemistry to become living cells, and ultimately people? This is a "bottom up" model of who we are and assumed by Evolutionists. One of a number of unresolved problems dogging it is where our consciousness would come from?

Or are we a "top down" product designed by an inventive consciousness of stupendous intelligence and power? If we are, then the problem of where our consciousness comes from disappears.

Or perhaps both processes are involved – Creation and Evolution?

In this book I present an entirely new "Theory of Creation" that resolves where you came from and why, and what your destiny is. Big call, I know, but providing you keep a thoughtful, open mind you will find it to be true.

Be prepared to change everything you thought you knew about Creation, Time and Evolution.

The truth is bigger and better than you previously believed. It is the doorway into discovering the meaning of Life, Time and Creation itself.

But beware—any new thinking even if scripturally sound may be easy to taste, but still be very hard to swallow, and we can automatically dismiss it without fair trial.

I am not saying God has not given similar perspectives to others, but I cannot find them written anywhere. Therefore, I have undertaken the daunting task of attempting to write and share them myself.

Once you have imbibed the essence of what I am presenting, you can expand on it, giving your own examples, perhaps in articles or books you write. In any case, please proclaim the fresh insights on social media.

I then move far beyond this fresh revelation that solves who we are and where we came from into probing the very nature of God—and dare to suggest how and why he does things, and what our destiny looks like.

Every book needs a hero. The hero of this book is God himself, and he is a superhero above all others, and an extraordinarily productive one until today!

And because there is only one God, then all elements of what exists, including the past, present and future, must somehow harmonise—as we discover they do.

The wonderful thing is that as original ancient scriptures are clarified, what Time *really* is emerges, and all the doctrinaire positions of Young Earth Creation, Old Earth Creation, Intelligent Design etc become feasible and perhaps even used by God during different stages of our present Universe's development. Each is at best a partial solution, while this book presents the full *Big Solution*.

We will also probe God's ongoing resourcefulness across a wide range that includes things he does innovatively on our planet to this day.

We will discover that God is surprisingly closer to aspects of ourselves than perhaps we had realised previously. There is a wonderful reason for this that emerges as we contemplate scripture and the extraordinary things he does.

Be prepared to be amazed – and thrilled.

How qualified am I to write this book about God and how he does things? I am not an expert in any of the areas I explore in the book you are about to read. It is different from most of my other 12 published books (see ivanrudolph.com), so I cannot claim much experience of writing in this field. However, I have an open and enquiring mind, and tenacity in research. The first of my university degrees majored in Geology and Chemistry, and I have continued my interest in these disciplines although a relative amateur in both. I have in addition closely investigated modern miracles, answered prayer, near death experiences (NDEs) and the fulfilment of divine prophecies. Each of these areas in which God is still actively involved on Earth has contributed to the startling revelations in these pages.

Our human nature and purpose in our world, and more especially our destiny, all emerged as I searched relentlessly for truth.

I hope you find it a stimulating and immensely helpful read.

INTRODUCTION

The Meaning of Life, Time and Creation

To probe for answers, I must enter controversial fields without apology. One of these, while not pivotal to the discussions, may be unfamiliar to many readers—that of Near Death Experiences (NDEs). I will start by describing briefly this extraordinary phenomenon, written about already by thousands and experienced by millions. A growing number of faithful Christian Ministers are admitting and informing us about their NDEs, as described in my previous book *"Living Beyond: Making Sense of Near Death Experiences"*.

Near Death Experiences

Ecclesiastes 12:7 describes death as, "The dust returns to the ground it came from, and the spirit returns to God who gave it". Simply put, a process is involved in this separation of the spirit from the body at death, and then its subsequent movement towards God. Scriptural truth is illuminated by the after-death accounts of those Near Death Experiencers (NDErs) who have returned to describe them.

Unusual insights about near death experiences were developed in *"Living Beyond"*. Since writing it, I have had the opportunity to reflect on whether the clarity that afterlife experiences reveal about God may contribute to shedding fresh light on how he creates things, including where and why we fit in. It has done so for me.

One obvious deduction from NDEs is that our fundamentally innovative God has made further Venues outside our own Universe, with novel characteristics and different physical, chemical and biological laws. I hope to share some of these exciting descriptions and what they mean to us.

NDErs, clinically dead and subsequently revived, have recorded an account of ongoing consciousness and experiences "out of this world". It has been estimated that at least 16 million Americans[2], excluding many children, have had a near death experience and are part of a large worldwide contingent of around 380 million adults[2]. With so many witnesses, any unbiased court of law would be forced to determine that NDEs are valid and indeed a common experience!

Here is a brief summary of the most common aspects of such experiences:

At death, our spirit (consciousness) floats out of the body and can view its earthly surroundings. It may then return to the body (physical revival) or move on to a series of afterlife activities and Venues. Amongst these events, it is common to meet with ancestors, angelic beings, God the Father or Jesus Christ—whether one enters the afterlife with any religion or none. The founders of religions other than Jesus and Christianity appear not to be met with.

A challenging experience can be a Life Review, when the dead person's life history is presented to them in astonishing detail—not as a Judgement, but rather as an opportunity for self-evaluation.

The centrality of "Family" to God is revealed in that thousands of reports describe having met ancestors in the afterlife. Sometimes these ancestors are not recognised by the NDEr as they had died long beforehand. Only discussions on return with older family members, or the scanning of ancient family photographs or portrait paintings, have enabled certain of these ancestors to be identified. Other "older" ancestors may remain unidentified to the experiencer.

After a while in the afterlife, the spirits of returnees come back into the body that was left behind, and their earthly life resumes. Sadly, many then experience trauma from unnecessary rejection by their families, friends, churches and professions.

At no stage do NDEs take precedence over the revelations of scripture in my life or my writing. The main innovative revelations in this book are independent of NDEs: on the other hand, NDEs add breadth to our understanding of both ourselves and of our God.

While important, NDEs are nevertheless recounted in the words of frequently confused and even traumatised witnesses who often put their own interpretations on what has happened to them. The accounts are strongest when simply describing what was seen or heard. They get their dependability from the size of the sample of millions of people who have had similar experiences.

Why consider NDEs? Because studied judiciously, they enhance our comprehension of the nature and creativity of God *beyond our own Universe*, which expands our perception of God's inventive genius, and consequently provides fresh insight into the Creation of our own Cosmos and our meaningful place in it.

Significantly for you and me, as well as for those who experience them, NDEs challenge our thinking as we try to unlock our own purpose—both past and future.

NDEs also illustrate that life on Earth is only a short blip in an ongoing process, but nevertheless an important opportunity for personal development not to be missed.

The Bible

My belief is that the Bible is an inspired gift from God and, correctly translated, has ultimate authority. The Bible is the main reference I have used, so I need to clarify from the start my approach to it.

I believe that the Bible is inerrant as inspired originally by the Holy Spirit in the original languages in which it was written—in the main these are biblical Hebrew (Old Testament) and biblical "Koine" Greek (Septuagint and New Testament).

Throughout history, Bible translators have done a magnificent job, often under conditions of poverty and persecution, and I have the greatest respect for them. They are true heroes of the faith, who continue today serving God and man by producing new translations of scripture for different language groups around the globe, at times under threat for their very lives. A girl I once taught in school is involved in distributing new translations of the Bible amongst language groups that have not had this wonderful resource previously—she is both brilliant and brave.

While translators continue to do valuable and frequently courageous work, we must keep aware that any translation from one language into another will lose precision and a degree of meaning. All our versions in modern languages, including the English language, are translations and are "dogged" (in the sense of being misconstrued in certain spots) by this linguistic limitation. Some of the more modern translations also produce sections of interpretation rather than accurate translation in an attempt to reflect the social mores of the day. I try not to quote these errant passages.

In whatever language, the Bible is a difficult book to interpret on some levels, but fortunately the Holy Spirit, who is our Teacher and who inspired scripture, is still available in our world for us to turn to prayerfully for help. You can trust him to reveal truth appropriate to your particular situation at the time, even if the words as translated have lost some precision by being written originally in a different language. He is, after all, the original inspirer of scripture and can make up any gap in your and my understanding.

Unfortunately, we can prefer to rely on our brainpower and consequently have invented intellectual approaches to interpret scripture, such as "hermeneutic analysis" and others, which often lead to confusion and disagreement. Why? Fundamentally—this is because the Bible is a spiritual revelation and requires a spiritual interpretation, as guided by the Holy Spirit. The brain cannot interpret the spirit, it is the other way around if meaningful interpretation is to occur at all.

Despite some linguistic perplexities, the overall messages and themes of the Bible are clear and unequivocal. God had mankind in mind, and had plans for us in place, before the first atom in our Universe was actually created!

God lays out clearly his nature and major purposes for humankind from Genesis to Revelation, such that there is no excuse for "twisting" anything important on the basis of a single word or phrase.

I have used the printed NIV (New International Version) for most quotes, unless I feel it is inaccurate or another version clarifies a passage better, in which case I indicate which alternative version has been used.

That I use the NIV is not to say that it is the best or most accurate version throughout, but it is generally good and written in readily accessible modern English—and is popular.

QUOTING THE BIBLE BOOK OF ISAIAH

The book I quote from most in the Old Testament besides Genesis is the Book of Isaiah. There is a specific and centrally important reason for this. The original was written around 700 BC, but a copy was found amongst the Dead Sea Scrolls in the 1940s, and has been carbon-dated to around 125 BC[3]. It is startling that there is no significant difference between this version that pre-dated Jesus' coming and what we read in our Bibles today—which were translated from much later scrolls, ones written around a thousand years after Christ! This illustrates how meticulous the scribes were who made copies of the scrolls down through the centuries.

The book of Isaiah is rich in information regarding humankind and our purposes, the Creation, and God as the Creator—alongside prophecies concerning the coming Messiah and other events that have taken place more recently in history. It is good to quote from, because sceptics cannot propose that the astonishingly exact details foretold about the life of Jesus and other events were written about *after* they had occurred!!

Using logic—because the book of Isaiah is incredibly, almost unnervingly, precise regarding the details of fulfilled prophecy—we can expect a similar degree of precision whenever it speaks of God's innovative nature and the Creation itself, and our own origins, purposes and futures, which it does in significant detail.

Besides the Psalms, Isaiah is the book most quoted from by the New Testament writers.

MY PERSONAL EMPHASES

Many of the ideas in this book are my own, and have not been published previously. By nature, we tend to reject new concepts when we first come across them, and so I may return to these more than once simply to clarify or apply them, but hopefully not too often for my readers.

Those of you who might like more detail, theology and referencing, please see my website ivanrudolph.com. I may be putting up relevant "free" material on it from time to time, mainly in response to emailed questions.

PART 1

WERE YOU CREATED?

OR DID YOU EVOLVE?

OR BOTH?

CHAPTER 1

QUESTIONING EVOLUTION

If you are truly confident about something, you welcome honest questions about it.

—Peter Kreeft[4]

I am uncomfortable about this chapter because it zeros in on me, one human unimportant to the debate—but I have been advised to keep it in, to enable you to relate to me as a fellow traveller. My search to find our ultimate origins is a common one that you too might share.

We cannot answer "Who Am I?" until we know where we ultimately came from, and *why*.

In addition, many who have trained in Science have been unsettled about the Creation and Evolution dispute, which was resolved for me over forty years ago. However, similar questions continue to trouble some of my friends and fellow Christians, becoming one important impetus for me to take on the challenge of writing this book.

———✦———

I grew up unchurched. Our family attended church I am told for weddings, funerals and christenings, but I don't remember any of these occasions—

except one. I have no memory of the church itself or the service, but it was a Greek Christening and afterwards we repaired to a hall where tables had been set with lavish food. I can still picture the bowls of coloured sugared almonds (pink and blue?) and sweet cakes. A deep and abiding impression had been made that church might be OK. A celebration that included special food. The way into a young boy's heart…

At school, I enjoyed both Science and History, which was an unusual combination. I have changed little over the intervening years. I also won a writing competition as a teenager with an account of "Rocks on Hitchhike" describing the specimens I had collected during a hitchhiking tour of the African countryside in Rhodesia, now named Zimbabwe. How times have changed; not many contemporary parents would welcome their young son hitchhiking and sleeping rough wherever the fancy took him. An interest in rocks and Geology had been birthed, together with the satisfaction of putting pen to paper.

When it came to choosing subjects for university I chose the Sciences over History because the job opportunities seemed more varied and interesting. Geology and Chemistry were my majors. Chemistry? Unusual perhaps, but I wanted a deep knowledge about the composition of substances, including the rocks I collected, and no other subject gave that. I have never regretted studying it—you'd be surprised how many meals I have rescued in our kitchen because of knowing Chemistry! Food again—definitely a way into my heart.

At university in the sixties, I became dubious about Evolutionary Theory. In Geology, I could see the progressive changes within a given species in the fossils we examined, but was unconvinced by the lack of fossils linking one species to another. We were mainly studying marine fossils, and the supposition was that fish supposedly arose from natural selection occurring in simpler life forms such as sea squirts. A keen fisherman, I felt such radical changes would involve a large number of successful "link" fossils with characteristics between fish and, say, the ancestral sea squirts—which are a crude invertebrate life form that attaches to a rock on the rocky shoreline—but neither did I see these link fossils, nor did the literature of that era identify any of them.

Natural selection was considered by Charles Darwin to bring profound changes from one species to the next step-by-step in a slow progression.

Thinking of the vertebrate fish I enjoyed catching, and eating, they were so different to a sea squirt that I found difficulty conceptualising what the link fossils would even look like. Sea squirt fossils had been found and likewise masses of fish fossils, but not as far as I could find out the hypothesised link fossils between sea squirts and fish. (Those were pre-Google days, so I tried again online recently–but still could not see any link fossils leading to fish!) Each of the link fossils would have survived, as I understood Darwinism, *only* if the changes it experienced had been favoured by the environmental conditions—so we might have expected masses of these successful new link fossils: not finding any of them made no sense to me.

My comprehension as a university student of what the Evolutionists were proposing was limited; but I am describing how I saw the problems at that phase. The same proved true for other supposed changes of one life form into another; there were too few if any successful link fossils. I was unconvinced. Nevertheless, I accepted the big picture of Darwinian Evolution, and began to read around the topic for additional insight about how this had actually happened.

Being the 1960s, the Watson and Crick model for the structure of DNA had been accepted, but its significance was in the infancy of understanding when applied to evolutionary theory. The variability within biological genetics, including the proposed contributions of epigenetics (external influences that affect genes) and of punctuated equilibrium (rapid change in life forms between long periods of little or no change), were at that juncture relatively understated or unknown—at least to the public and myself.

Because he was essentially the founding father of Evolutionary Theory, it was appropriate for me to read about Charles Darwin[5] and some of the things he proposed. This was not done in a rush but in bits and pieces.

While not a committed Christian at that stage, I am now and have recently read some Christian material that denigrated Darwin and his conclusions. From reading Darwin's own words, which most Christians have not done, I respect him as a meticulous and thoughtful Scientist. Scientists should be encouraged to put forward theories to try to explain observations they have made, even if their hypotheses prove unpopular. They and others then set about investigating to what extent these fledgling concepts might be valid and trustworthy. Fundamentally, many aspects of Darwin's assumptions involving Evolution have been demonstrated relatively successfully. Not many other theories proposed before 1860 have survived nearly as well! Nevertheless, because his theory cannot explain convincingly certain complexities regarding life and life forms, and the initiation of life itself, it is at best only one part of a greater truth. Even in his day with its limited knowledge, Darwin was frustrated when trying to explain the intricacies and interdependence of parts of the human eye.

> To suppose that the eye with all its inimitable contrivances for adjusting the focus for different distances, for admitting different amounts of light, and for the correction of spherical and chromatic aberration, could have been formed by natural selection seems, I freely confess, absurd in the highest degree.

He goes on to state it could have happened, provided each small helpful physical change could be passed on to succeeding generations. Nowadays we know that the inheritance of physical changes does not happen with quite the facility and precision that Darwin hoped, and we know hugely more about the interdependent complexity of the structure and functioning of the human eye—which is dependent on a separate visual centre in the brain, tear glands and tears with just the right chemical mix and alkalinity, three primary colour cones to mix light stimuli into all the colours we see and enjoy, protective eye sockets and eyelids and so much else besides—such that what Darwin described as apparently "absurd in the highest degree" is certainly "profoundly absurd".

In addition, our escalating knowledge of Microbiology and the interdependence and complexity of all living systems makes any unguided process of development appear less and less likely—and our biochemical knowledge of this interdependence is burgeoning. Even as a student, I already recognised a number of complex biochemical systems unlikely to have arisen spontaneously.

This question of spontaneous development of life itself from non-living materials appeared to have been given a boost in experiments that duplicated the chemical soup supposed to have existed on a primordial Earth—and when energy was added, some amino acids were produced. Now amino acids are the building blocks for proteins, which can self-replicate, and it was assumed the first life forms could have been generated by a similar process. My conceptual understanding of Chemistry made me doubt this, amino acids being non-living, and light years from an independent living cell—the brown bottles of amino acids on the shelves of laboratories around the world had shown no signs of generating a life form, according to people who had inspected them hopefully. Furthermore, what I had learnt at school about a "simple cell" as the building block of life was no longer considered simple at all, but more like a village where each member was sustained by interactions with others and the environment. (Currently, the "simple cell" is recognised as extraordinarily complex and now more like an interdependent city!)

Logically, I questioned whether all this could have arisen spontaneously simply by chance interactions involving comparatively simple scientific laws?

When a previous theory is no longer capable of explaining complex observations, a new theory is called for, or at least a radical readjustment of the old one. Back then, I decided to question my esteemed Professor of Geology, Geoffrey Bond, regarding my doubts.

The Professor listened patiently to me. He agreed that no mechanism or combination of mechanisms so far suggested by scientists could explain the appearance and development of life on Earth. I was surprised how readily he agreed to this. However, he made a vital point: while mechanisms remained mysterious, nevertheless the stages of the development of the different life forms in the fossil record were recorded internationally and there could be no doubt about this progressive development. The big picture of past Evolution had definitely happened. What remained elusive was a mechanism to explain *how* these evolutionary changes were brought about.

He left me with a suggestion that captured my thinking for a while. "I think the scientists investigating how life may have begun are not taking sufficient notice of the millions of years involved. I think the solution to these problems lies in the Time factor."

For more than a year, the input of Time into the quest for a mechanism to explain Evolution satisfied me. Time was the missing factor, but of course one almost impossible to test reliably in the laboratory.

Towards the end of my university degree, I became unsure all over again when I looked at my chaotic desk with books, pages of notes, pens, pencils, stapler, paper punch, some medications, scraps of paper and all sorts of things scattered higgledy-piggledy over the surface. I felt that for the desk items to become sorted again after exams, it would take me to do it. My *conscious intelligence* would have to be involved to produce rational order, not simply blind natural forces—regardless of how many billions of years my desk might be left to the mercy of visionless forces.

As I pondered my chaotic desk, I began to question my Professor's reliance on Time and unintelligent random forces for producing and guiding the systematic development of increasingly complex life forms on the planet.

And where did these original forces described by elegant Physics equations come from anyway? To construct the Cosmos, did they pre-exist the proposed Big Bang? Otherwise, could a chaotic explosive Big Bang have produced them?

My confidence in Time as a complete explanation for the appearance and development of life became uncertain. Time to me most likely played a part, but no matter how many years were involved, I simply could no longer conceptualise life itself arising naturally out of extreme primordial chaos. I decided instead that design input by a conscious intelligence must have been involved somehow.

That was my thought-out conclusion.

I knew that within a given species, using selective breeding, the intervention of human intelligence made it possible to produce a multiplicity of varieties very quickly, essentially by copying the routes of natural selection. Nevertheless, despite the thousands of breeding experiments over the years, the many varieties of dogs remained dogs, and of cattle remained cattle. Not even one had definitely changed into another species as far as I could find out from my questioning and reading.

In nature, natural selection produces variety within a breed, but more slowly and with less variation than conscious human intelligence has achieved. I believed while at university that natural selection was a valid concept, and still do—but became unsure that it could have launched life itself.

What is more, the lack of multiple link fossils made me wonder whether natural selection could in reality change one species into another very different one, as Darwin had supposed it had done already many times. Instead, it now seemed to me that the input of an external organising intelligence remained an essential addition to the evolutionary development of new species, and of life itself.

My questioning had nothing to do with religion; nor was I a follower of any religion or any spiritual leader. In fact, during this period of uncertainty I sadly talked a childhood friend out of his Catholicism and into atheism, which I considered the more logical path. He is an atheist to this day.

Some people reading this may wonder why I was searching for answers seeing that I was not spiritually involved? It's just my nature I guess. I am a natural seeker after truth, always have been since very young. I don't like to be ignorant nor conned and never accept things without a lot of questions, questions, QUESTIONS—which others can find very wearying. A good friend staying with us scolded me in frustration, "Too many questions!"

The end of university days came in a rush without the opportunity, time or inclination to think further about how life could have begun.

Soon it became necessary because of family reasons to find work near Umtali (now Mutare in Zimbabwe). The only suitable employment available there was as a Science Teacher because becoming a Geologist (my preferred choice) would have necessitated much time spent in the bush.

Shortly afterwards I married Brenda, my wonderful wife to this day, and the demands of establishing myself in my new profession and taking sporting teams over weekends, as well as playing my own sport, left me with less than zero opportunity to pursue the riddle of life appearing and developing on Earth. This problem was like a stew "left on the back burner" of a stove.

And there it remained until my late twenties, when a series of unexpected events overtook me and my jumble of questions bubbled over again.

CHAPTER 2

THE INSPIRED ANSWER

In a time of universal deceit—telling the truth is a revolutionary act.

—George Orwell[6]

When converted to Christianity in my late-twenties, I was filled with wonder at the reality of God, something I had never expected because of my secular background.

I came into an authentic relationship with God outside of the church and it took a while before I discovered that church attendance could be helpful. Meanwhile, I enjoyed regular fellowship with a group of friends and attended different Christian meetings that came my way.

I perceived conflicting viewpoints between what I had learned as a Geology student and what many Christians believed about the Creation of the world and the life forms on it. I was convinced that the world had come about by a slow growth process over millions of years, while some Christian friends believed it to be a special act of 6-day Creation only a few thousand years ago. What I had learnt in Geology, and what I had seen for myself on field trips, made this "Young-Earth Creation" model for the Earth and Cosmos seem preposterous.

For example, I pondered the extensive bedding layers in sedimentary rocks separated by discontinuities representing epochs of erosion rather than deposition, and then new beds of sediments deposited on top again, sometimes at different angles because of folding of the first sediments, and these sequences repeated time and again. I had inspected examples of these discontinuities myself in the bush. Where comparable sediments occur in the present era, significant expanses of Time have passed.

And what about the varved clays which sedimented out differently summer to winter such that they illustrated annual seasons similar to the growth rings on trees? Bell Canyon varves alone would indicate deposition for around 260000 years and those in the American Green Shales an even longer period of formation. Yet some Christians seemed to suggest all this had happened during the short crisis of Noah's flood—which seemed unreasonable. But most things about God were brand new to me; therefore, I remained open to be convinced otherwise.

Happily, I had by then enjoyed some very definite real and personal experiences with God, such that my belief in him was confirmed experientially and was not immediately shaken by these seemingly "wild" Christian theories about the origin of the Universe and of life on our planet. Experience always trumps theory, for me at least.

Were my Christian friends deceived, then, about the nature of the Creation? This did not seem likely, as they were knowledgeable about God and generally sensible about life. They were intelligent, educated professional and business people. While my belief in God was secure, my knowledge about him and how he did things was at a very formative stage.

Slowly, uncertainty crept in. I began to question the things I had learned in Geology and other branches of Science. This indecision troubled me over a period of weeks.

At one of our fellowship meetings, a man I highly respected told us how God had given him some answers he had needed, through reading the Bible. He had first prayed, then opened the Bible to random pages and spent a while reading, during which process his questions had been answered. In common with my friend and millions of others, I had already found that God communicated things personally during the prayerful reading of scripture, so I decided to ask God to show me similarly, also from a relevant scripture reading, the answers to my questions. I am not recommending this as a substitute for serious study or an example to be followed; I am simply recording what happened in my life on that occasion.

I spent a while on my knees beside my bed asking God to show me how he had created the Universe. I had no doubt that he had done so. None whatsoever. The mystery was—*how* had he done so and over what time period? I told God that if he showed me it was all in 6-days, and that was all there was to it, I would accept that and question it no further. It was in this attitude of faith and total willingness to change my views that I opened the Bible at random and began to read.

The verse I opened to was thrilling and came with insight that resolved my problem.

I have been hesitant to describe this here, because it may appear that I am claiming that "because God showed me, it is the complete truth and don't you dare disagree." Not at all! My experience is that while God may initiate fresh insight on a certain topic, he still intends for us to forage and learn more. As Jesus instructed,

> Keep asking, and it will be given to you. Keep searching, and you will find. Keep knocking, and the door will be opened for you. Because everyone who keeps asking will receive, and the person who keeps searching will find, and the person who keeps knocking will have the door opened. (Matthew 7:7-8 quoted from the International Standard Bible.)

The above translation provides the true emphasis in the original biblical Greek, using the *present imperative* tense that implies continuity of activity.

God had given me personally a satisfying answer that thrilled me. It became a foundation for the development of my further studies. These have informed my ongoing deeper comprehension of God and his creativity—and over the years became the inspiration for this book.

On my knees all those years ago, I had opened my King James translation of the Bible at Psalm 139. Verses 15 and 16 jumped out at me:

> My substance was not hid from Thee, when I was made in secret, and curiously wrought in the lowest parts of the Earth. Thine eyes did see my substance, yet being imperfect; and in Thy book all my members were written, which in continuance were fashioned, when as yet there was none of them.

Several things struck me immediately.

*The words "curiously wrought" suggested there is a mystery to how God makes a person.

*The phrase "in the lowest parts of the Earth", suggested life may have a derivation or formation linked to the Earth itself, as claimed by Evolution.

*The most important and life-changing expression to me was "in Thy book all my members (body parts) were written (decided) **which in continuance were fashioned, when as yet there was none of them**".

The words "***in continuance** were fashioned,*" pointed to a process, not to an instantaneous action. Most significantly, "when as yet there was ***none*** of them", indicated to me that we pre-exist in some pre-planned stage, even if just in God's mind in Heaven, before we actually appear on Earth. I saw at once a detailed two-stage plan, with "in Thy book" referring to God's pre-planning of the psalmist's life before he was humanly conceived on Earth.

I perceived that God's acts of Creation described in Genesis would also have likely occurred first in Heaven "when as yet there were *none* of them" in our Universe. Their subsequent appearance in our world could then happen over whatever timing God chose. This could be consistent with an evolving Creation.

The immediate insight and comprehension I gained all those years ago gelled for me into the foundational principle of God's design and implementation.

God can choose to create in Two Stages:

First stage in Heaven
Later stages on Earth.

For simplicity, I term this God's "Two-Stage Process".

Tragically, the way that God often does things has never been fully understood either by Bible translators nor by Christians in general, contributing to the pitiful morass that Christianity is in today with so many unnecessary variations of doctrines. Conflicting teachings on Evolution and Creation are firmly in this unwarranted category.

There is debate amongst scholars (which goes without saying) over what these verses in Psalm 139 might mean and different Bible translations use different wording. For example, the NIV and most others write "days" instead of "members", which gives the startling, "All the *days* ordained for me were written in Your book before one of them came to be". This alternative would make it even clearer that we pre-exist in God's plan in Heaven before we are formed on Earth. It would also go some distance to explain the common expression recorded by hundreds of NDErs, i.e. returnees from a Near Death Experience, who have been told they were being sent back to Earth because "Your *Time* is not yet".

Suffice to say that the instant interpretation I received on my knees does not depend upon which version of the Bible is read. More importantly, it is absolutely consistent with what we find in other parts of scripture, if we forage for ourselves, especially in the sections of the Bible that are seldom taught.

Even today, God personally does many things on our planet that do not involve Evolution—such as answered prayer, miracles, fulfilment of ancient biblical prophecies, and other actions that we will look at in this book, starting with one miracle in this next chapter that reveals something extraordinary about God and Time.

CHAPTER 3

PONDERING ONE MIRACLE OF HEALING

MIRACLES are a retelling in small letters of the very same story which is written across the whole world in letters too large for some of us to see.

—C. S. Lewis[7]

The rest of this book is written through the prism of understanding that God plans all sorts of things first in Heaven, then implements his plans afterwards in our Universe and in our lives on Earth—"Two-Stage Theory".

My appreciation of this has developed over the years; I see it as seminal to comprehending scripture and reconciling aspects of both Creation and Evolution. Furthermore, it helps us to comprehend more deeply the nature of God and his involvement with us through Time—past, present, future—and into eternity.

Learning to apply Two-Stage Theory to the Bible is essential to grasp who we are and what we are doing here. In part because Christian denominations do not know about Two-Stage Theory, we have unnecessarily confusing doctrinal positions and, tragically, thousands of different Christian denominations. Christian theology is obviously in a lot of trouble.

I have always found that Time is a pivotal variable in probing how God does things—Time on Earth and Time in Heaven. It is so important that I often capitalise it, as I do other words when wanting to draw attention to them.

But we need to keep in mind that Time on Earth is a simplified version of Time as recorded in the Bible. This is the heart of why Scientists do not know what Time truly is, because on our planet we only experience a small part of the whole picture. Think of your favourite painting, perhaps the Mona Lisa by da Vinci, or the Night Watch by Rembrandt, and suppose you had only ever been shown a tiny albeit artistic segment taken from the whole artwork, how could you possibly conceptualise the grandeur and complexity of the overall painting? That is why we cannot in our world define nor comprehend what Time, Consciousness, Love, Energy and other vital aspects of our existence are! The "big picture", and a more comprehensive revelation, awaits us in the afterlife!

However, we can while still on our planet do better than we have done previously. To do so is massively, stupendously, to your advantage, and to mine.

I have heard the erroneous opinion that "Miracles don't happen nowadays" given by armchair experts. My response is always the same: "Why not go and investigate for yourself? Find local churches where they pray in faith for the sick and ask the Ministers to describe miracles that have happened. Then set up interviews with those that have been healed and decide whether they would be good witnesses in a court of law. Ask to copy any physical confirmation that might be proffered, such as x-rays taken before and after the miracle, letters from medical personnel and so on."

I did just that myself. Not only did I discover miracles happening nowadays, with absolutely convincing medical evidence to back them up, but I had opened a fresh window into appreciating aspects of God and his nature. I will share some of these discoveries later in this book.

Right now, I am going to give a detailed description of just one of a number of miracles that captured my investigative attention as a new

Christian, because it clearly illustrates how God can and does do some things far quicker on Earth than we might anticipate.

Graeme Stokes was a young boy in Rhodesia (now Zimbabwe). I first saw him when I was attending a Pentecostal church there in the mid-1970s and he and his parents came to the front of the church to describe Graeme's recent miracle healing. Graeme's mother described how her son had been struggling with a dental condition called a "bulldog bite" for some years. The family had come to Salisbury (now Harare) to have it treated during the school holidays. Hearing of the extraordinary healing miracles that were happening at this particular church, which had even been reported in the local newspaper, the Stokes family had decided to come for prayer the Sunday before the scheduled appointment with their Dentist, Dr Bowker. Dr Bowker had previously discussed with them the radical intervention that was needed to treat Graeme's bulldog bite, and that a minimum of six months would be required for the correction.

At the appropriate juncture in that service, Pastor Bill Anstruther had invited those who would like to be prayed for to come forward. Graeme had gone out to the front along with his mother. When the Pastor had laid a hand on the youngster's head and prayed for him, people nearby heard a loud cracking sound. Startled, they looked at Graeme, to see that his jaw line had changed. The bulldog bite had disappeared completely! They had witnessed a rare instantaneous reconstruction miracle. There was a lot of excitement and thankfulness to the Lord among the congregation.

At the close of the service I sought out Graeme and his parents. I had a special request; would they be prepared to go back to their Dentist for him to verify the miracle? As a Christian with scientific training, I had begun investigating the rash of miracles that were happening at this little church, but I liked to have documentation before telling other people about them. Although surprised by my request, the parents agreed to do this for me.

Dr Bowker, a highly qualified and reputable Dental Surgeon, practised from smart rooms in the prestigious precinct for Doctors and Dentists in that era—North Avenue. I met with Graeme and Mrs Stokes before they went in to see him and took some photos of Graeme, especially of his now perfect jaw line.

They were in the Dentist's rooms for a while. I waited outside.

When they emerged, Mrs Stokes was smiling broadly. "Dr Bowker didn't believe it was Graeme at first. He told his Nurse that she must have brought him the wrong card. The Nurse told him it was definitely the correct one and he looked very confused. Graeme told him that he had been prayed for and healed, and I added that I'd very much like a letter from him to confirm this. Dr Bowker's face went all funny and he plopped down into his chair. We all looked at him and waited for him to say something, but he was speechless. It's the first time I've seen someone actually speechless; I didn't know it really happened."

"How long did he stay like that?" I asked, surprised at the Dentist's unexpected reaction.

"I didn't check my watch. Some minutes, at least," Mrs Stokes replied.

I smiled, but had to ask what was uppermost on my mind. "Did he verify the miracle?"

"Yes, he did. He first of all re-examined Graeme. Then he told us the healing was perfect and that he was amazed. He questioned Graeme further. Finally, he said he would prepare a letter for me to collect later."

Here follows a copy of that letter, which is still in my possession. I would like to commend Dr Bowker for providing it. Many of his colleagues would not have been prepared to record on paper their scientific observations of a miracle for fear of ridicule. Of course, true Scientists are not afraid of facts and do not ignore or hide them, but are prepared to record them. (Incidentally, in this regard, Charles Darwin's reports accord with true Science).

40 North Avenue
Salisbury
Rhodesia.
Telephone: 20981

Dr. O.B. Bowker
B.D.S. (RAND)
DENTAL SURGEON

18th November, 1975.
REF: OBB/JRB.

Dear Mrs. Stokes,

With reference to our conversation yesterday about your son Graeme, I am only too delighted to place the following facts on record:

1. As you will remember I examined Graeme on the 25th July 1975 and as well as informing you that he required a number of fillings we also discussed the problem of his bite. Without going into too many technical details, suffice it to say that when he closed his teeth together the relationship between the top front teeth and the lower front teeth was the reverse of what they should be, i.e. he had a "Bulldog" type bite relationship. I proposed that I make him an appliance to correct this malocclusion and I estimated it would take between 6 months to 1 year to correct his bite.

2. Graeme returned for his treatment on 13th November, 1975 and much to my amazement his bite was perfectly normal and, at one stage, I even questioned my Nurse as to whether the treatment card I had was the correct one. Graeme, on being questioned about his teeth, said "I asked a man to pray for me and he fixed my teeth". To repeat, I am delighted to have been able to see this divine cure for myself.

Yours sincerely,

[signature]

What, you may wonder, has this account of a miracle healing long ago got to do with the topic of God's creativity?

For one thing, it demonstrates that God *still* intervenes *creatively*, as has been attested by miracles around the world before and since. I still possess x-rays from that period of my research which demonstrate two further ingenious miracles beyond reasonable medical doubt.

Miracles illustrate that God did not stop creating after he had designed and formed the Cosmos during those six days of productive brilliance in Heaven, as described in Genesis. He has continued to create miraculously ever since.

And when God does miracles, he displays his mastery over Time and circumstance.

As I pondered the Graeme Stokes incident, I imagined myself in Dr Bowker's shoes and conjectured what might have caused his strange speechless reaction to the miracle. Could it be that standing in front of him was a patient who pointed back to a prayer experience of a few seconds that had achieved what would otherwise have required a minimum of six months' dental treatment? Perhaps Dr Bowker's previous experience with dental treatments and the Time needed for them had been shaken?

Much more significant for us is that the incident illustrated whatever usually takes a long Time on our planet can happen in seconds, should God so choose. God has absolute control over Time on Earth and how long his actions will take. We estimate the Time needed for an event from our previous worldly experiences, but locked into our physical Cosmos as we are, we simply do not know how long God may have taken over creating what we see.

So, let's apply this new understanding to the Creation with God having planned it first in Heaven, in a different Time frame, before later forming our Universe with ourselves in it.

These ingenious processes might have played out very quickly—or very slowly—we cannot judge this absolutely. This variable nature of Time means that Young Earth Creation, Old Earth Creation, Intelligent Design and other models for Creation all become feasible and perhaps even used by God during different stages of the universe's actual development—a kind of "punctuated" growth.

As for myself, I believe the evidence from nature supports more strongly that an Old-Earth Creation and guided Evolution were the likely *main players*, but by no means exclusively so, in implementing God's innovative designs planned in Heaven from "in the beginning".

Analysis to find *where* an action occurs, in Heaven or on our planet, becomes critical to the interpretation of the timing and details of that particular event.

Unless "Venue" is determined *first*, the timing of events as we conceptualise them becomes unreliable. Sadly, many Christians including Bible commentators and translators have neither comprehended nor allowed for this.

For example, the six days of creating in Genesis 1 were describing the planning sequences taking place in days *in Heaven*, where God dwells, works and took a rest on the seventh heavenly day. Confusion and apparent contradictions and huge inaccuracies result from trying to interpret heavenly days and activities as though they were earthly ones.

Heavenly days and earthly days? Completely scriptural.

There is a very exciting fundamental reason for the terminology "days" to be used in the Bible for both Heaven and our world, which will be pursued in depth later. It will make your heart sing—as it does mine!

It is interesting that all three persons of the Trinity (God the Father, God the Son [Jesus] and God the Holy Spirit) were involved in Heaven in conceiving and creating the Universe, and would all three remain intimately involved in the unfolding history of our world, where our human experience of Time is linked to the sun and stars in our Cosmos.

What is heavenly Time linked to? We don't know yet, but certainly not to the sun and stars in our Universe even in advance of their being created! Yet this unsustainable interpretation is given to the "days of Creation" in Genesis by many theologians and Creationists.

The true nature of Time is essential for us to comprehend before we can grasp our origins. If Scientists cannot tell us what Time *really* is, can the inspired ancient spiritual insights in the Bible bridge the gap in our understanding?

For this to happen, we must distinguish what originates from God, working in Heaven, from what occurs *subsequently* on Earth.

Time is simply another variable that God uses resourcefully.

Mysteries about Time are unlocked as we ponder the scriptures. For example, Hebrew scholars translated biblical Hebrew into Greek two or more centuries before the birth of Christ, and we may safely assume those Hebrew translators knew far more about ancient Hebrew than our modern scholars do. The first books of the Old Testament in "koine" Greek that resulted, including Genesis, was termed the Septuagint and was not influenced by popular Cosmology such as our inaccurate modern translations have been. The Septuagint stuck more precisely to the tenses of past, present and future—and translates Genesis 2:3, "And God blessed the seventh day and sanctified it, because in it he ceased from all his works, *which God began to do*".

> *God BEGAN to do!! Only Two-Stage Theory and God's implementation on Earth of his heavenly plans made previously during the Creation week can explain "God BEGAN to do" satisfactorily.*

Genesis 2:3 shows that Creation has *never* stopped—it continues to be implemented in our Cosmos, and in our lives, to this very day.

A host of exciting revelations about Time and God are opened by this understanding that God's plans in Heaven are implemented later on Earth.

Prophecy (foretelling by God) functions in the same fashion—it is also planned first by God in Heaven, and then implemented later on Earth in a process of fulfillment that maps out your destiny and my destiny. Studying this enhances our understanding of Time and how God creates. Consequently, we will start to examine fulfilled prophecy in the next chapter.

PART 2

TIME ON EARTH
AND TIME IN HEAVEN

CHAPTER 4

GLIMMERINGS OF TIME

Science cannot tell Theology how to construct a doctrine of Creation, but you can't construct a doctrine of Creation without taking account of the age of the Universe and the evolutionary character of cosmic history.

—John Polkinghorne[8]

When events happened on Earth, and how long they took, is a major point of difference between Young-Earth Creationists, Geologists, Evolutionists, Biologists, Anthropologists – and others.

Our language is abundant with phrases about Time: having a good time; time of our lives; free time, ahead of their time, biding our time, keeping time, making time, from time to time etc. This richness is extraordinary considering we do not know what Time *really* is!!

We can be helped enormously in considering the nature of Time by recognising its existence outside our limited Universe.

There are remarkable Venues outside our Cosmos in which a form of Time exists. Our consciousness (spirit) travels to some of these once we die. We have now thousands of descriptions provided by Near Death Experiencers to work with, including those given by scientists, medical professionals and others who have been trained in making careful, unbiased observations and applying objective analysis. These Venues they describe illustrate that different laws and relationships exist outside our Cosmos.

Now here is the rub: Time, Energy, Consciousness and Love all exist outside our Universe in presentations "similar but different" to how we experience them on our planet.

These "new" (to us) presentations are generally more complex and fascinating, such that we can while on Earth readily embrace only simplified versions of them.

At once we can see why it is impossible on Earth to grasp fully what each of these mysterious fundamentals of our earthly existence are! Our experience of them is trivial and simplistic compared to their fulness, similar to a baby playing with a toy truck in the home—that baby can recognise trucks on the roads outside but cannot yet comprehend what a truck is in all its complexity and how it functions.

Time outside our Cosmos appears to follow expanded laws and principles, but is similar enough for Near Death Experiencers to have felt reasonably orientated to it in afterlife Venues. Nevertheless, because Time is so "advanced" there compared to what we have here, we cannot visualise its true extent and nature while still in our more limited Universe. We are like an ant crawling up an elephant's leg; that ant is too limited to comprehend the elephant's nature, function or inner biology. Similarly, we cannot as yet comprehend fully what Time is.

Perhaps one further analogy will help to clarify this.

To the world's surprise, a tribe of Western Desert Aborigines in Australia was found in 1984 that had never previously seen or heard of white people. The BBC reported in Outlook:

> In 1984 a group of Australian Aboriginal people living a traditional nomadic life were encountered in the heart of the Gibson desert in Western Australia. They had been unaware of the arrival of Europeans on the continent, let alone cars–or even clothes.

Imagine if, in the years prior to their first contact, this tribe had found a metal horse stirrup lying on desert sand, lost by an explorer riding across the desert years before. There are accounts similar to this in early literature when the tribe would gather around the mysterious article and discuss it. Perhaps it had fallen from the sky? What was it? What might it be used for?

Despite long deliberations, they could not possibly deduce accurately the function of the stirrup, because they had no experience of riding horses and knew nothing of horses at all. Horses were absolutely outside their world. We are in a similar position regarding Time which exists outside our world.

The same is true of Consciousness, Energy and Love. They were all imported into our world in a simplified form when God created it. Each has been included and adapted for us on Earth, and each is based on what already exists outside our ambience in afterlife Venues. Like the metal stirrup, each has a fuller expression and function *outside our Universe* than we could possibly comprehend right now! God's revelation to man is the only possible way for us to glimpse meaningfulness in such intangibles. Science depends on logic and intuition, but can take us only a short distance in our journey towards a more comprehensive understanding because at present it is restricted to studies within our limited Universe.

Christians see the writings that comprise the Bible as God's inspired gift to us in these matters. Regarding Time, for example, the first sentence in Genesis reads: "In the *beginning*, God created the heavens and the Earth", which tells us that Time pre-existed what he was creating. This is confirmed elsewhere, such as in Psalm 90:2:

> Before the mountains were born
> or you brought forth the whole world,
> from everlasting to everlasting you are God.

1Peter1:20 teaches:

> He (Jesus) was chosen **before** the Creation of the world, but was revealed in these last times for your sake.

Consider John 17:5. Shortly before Jesus' crucifixion, he prayed aloud to his Father in Heaven:

> "And now, Father, glorify me in your presence with the glory I had with you ***before*** the world began".

In addition, this verse reveals that prior to the Earth's formation, Jesus shared the glory of God the Father in Heaven. He then left to join us on Earth, so there was a period of Time during which Heaven was without him. After his death and resurrection, he returned to reside again with his Father in Heaven.

There is no sensible scriptural reason to doubt that Time exists in Heaven outside our Universe and preceded its Creation.

What the Bible reveals about Time and God's timings has helped to clarify for me the Creation itself and our roots—who we are, and why, flows from this understanding.

I found God's inspiration of scriptural wording to be very precise. Statements about what was to occur in the future (prophecy) were played out exactly as predicted. These include major events such as the 70-year captivity of the Jews in Babylon and a 400-year wait before the Israelites could possess the Promised Land.

Can we doubt that Heaven, where God lives, is where he plans our future, including our personal times and timings? It is as we found in Psalm 139, that our times are in His hands.

The only alternative is for future events and time lines described by prophets to be just lucky guesses.

Let's take a few predictions about ancient Tyre and challenge ourselves to guess how they were later fulfilled in history, providing you do not already know the historical answers of course. If you guess accurately without prior knowledge how God fulfilled this prophecy, you will have done better than upwards of 200 adults to whom I have set this as a challenge. Not one of them succeeded, but then neither had I!

We'll start with some historical facts:

"Old Tyre" as the ancient Greeks referred to it, was a very wealthy large Mediterranean city on the coastline of what is now modern Lebanon. It had a further lesser settlement on an island a kilometre or so across deep water. This island settlement was small, around five kilometres in circumference, but with two good ports.

The people of Tyre had proven to be implacable enemies of the Israelites. God inspired the prophet Ezekiel around 586 Bc to make a series of predictions against Tyre, all of which were fulfilled over Time to the letter.

Here are just four of them (Ezekiel 26):
1. Verse 3 – "I will bring many nations against you".
2. Verse 4 – "They will destroy the walls of Tyre and pull down her towers; I will scrape away her rubble and make her a bare rock."
3. Verse 12 – "They will break down your walls and demolish your fine houses and throw your stones, timber and rubble into the sea."
4. Verse 14 – "You will never be rebuilt, for I the Lord have spoken", declares the Sovereign Lord.

When we look at a map of the Middle East today, we see Tyre *still exists* in Lebanon on the shores of the eastern Mediterranean Sea. Is the prophecy still unfulfilled? Maybe it was only partially correct?

Historical records set the scene. Many nations did come against Tyre over the years, including the Egyptians, Assyrians, Persians, Babylonians and Greeks. King Nebuchadnezzar of Babylon, specifically named in the prophecy, did attack Tyre—laying siege to the city for twelve years and breaking down its walls and towers as foretold. However, the Tyrians fled across the sea to their offshore island, taking much of their wealth with them. Nebuchadnezzar commanded a predominantly land army and had no practical means of transporting it across to the island. After his siege, it has been suggested that the Tyrians sued for peace by presenting Nebuchadnezzar with some tokens of their incredible wealth to forestall future attacks, promising to be a vassal city loyal to him. In any case, for whatever reason, he marched away, leaving behind the tumbled down ruins of ancient Tyre.

Surviving Tyrians, from their island sanctuary, rejoiced as they watched Nebuchadnezzar and his army depart.

How do you think God might have fulfilled verse 4? "I will scrape away her rubble and make her a bare rock."

Maybe an earthquake? But the upheaval of earthquakes does not leave a scene of devastation as bare as a rock. Perhaps volcanic action would cover the ancient city with lava that solidified into rock after ancient Tyre's walls and houses were demolished and the rubble thrown into the sea?

While you are thinking, here are a few more details. The Tyrians, being a seafaring people, had a good fleet and felt secure on their island, and so did not rebuild Old Tyre from the ruins on the mainland. Instead, they bolstered the island defences with underwater reefs cunningly constructed and placed, such that they would not get covered by sand, but would dash to pieces any ships of an invading fleet.

It was over 200 years before the remaining prophecies regarding Tyre were fulfilled. This fits consistently into the pattern that many years of earthly Time may pass before a plan formulated by God in Heaven, even one revealed to man, is completed on our planet.

Alexander the Great came in 332 BC with his marauding Greek troops. The islanders scorned his threats to conquer them, and in fact butchered his messengers in full view on the walls of their island haven, disembowelling some and tossing their bodies into the sea. Not only did Alexander want the immense wealth of the Tyrians, he did not want to leave such a vicious, powerful enemy in his wake with its two good ports for hostile Persian ships to use (coming against him) while he was marching further south. However, he at once realised his small fleet would be damaged by the underwater rocky reefs. His ships could only encircle the island to prevent Tyrian ships escaping. He could not conquer Tyre from the sea.

What should he do?

Greek history tells us precisely what he did.

A brilliant strategist, despite knowing it would be a difficult and tedious procedure, Alexander devised an extraordinary and unique plan of attack. He set his army to dismantle the ancient ruins of Tyre on the mainland and cast her stones, timbers, rubble and even soil into the sea (verse 12)—and slowly built a causeway across the sea towards the island fortress. The causeway was a minimum of 60 metres wide, giving width enough to carry his fearsome army over it in breadth as well as depth.

Ultimately, Alexander succeeded in his conquest and put 10,000 Tyrians to the sword and sold 30,000 as slaves.

His causeway still exists today and has joined the island city of modern Tyre to the mainland. Modern Tyre thereby is no longer sits on an island; Alexander's causeway has turned it into a peninsula.

Old Tyre, though, was never rebuilt (verse 14).

How did you do? Tyre is the only known case where an ancient city not only ceased to exist but was flattened as a result of its stones, timbers, and even rubble being cast into the sea, leaving it a bare rock—precisely as foretold in the Bible. These events were recorded by the pagan Greeks in their own history.

What I learnt from this is that common sense, logic and flights of imagination are all inadequate in attempting to deduce God's fulfilment of anything in scripture, least of all the Creation plans outlined in such broad terms in Genesis 1. There is no room here for any Christian arrogance regarding times, methods or epochs.

Professor Stoner[9] and his students investigated the fulfilment of seven of the predicted details about Tyre that are historically verifiable. The team tackled the question as to whether Ezekiel could have made lucky guesses of what would happen to Tyre in the future. They used probability theory and very conservative estimates. I will quote from his book:

If Ezekiel had looked at Tyre in his day and had made these predictions in human wisdom, these estimates mean that there would have been only one chance in 75,000,000 of their all coming true. They all came true, in the minutest detail.

If you backed a horse with the odds of winning of 1 in 75,000,000—how much money would you gamble on it? Keep it small; that horse is not going to win! Or if a surgeon told you that your chances of surviving a particular operation were only 1 in 75,000,000, would you be happy to go ahead? Yet those who disbelieve there to be a God in control of biblical prophecies, and thereby of their own future, are taking a chance much greater than this magnitude. Hundreds of other prophecies have already been fulfilled in history and only a handful remain before Christ returns physically to Earth to wind-up life here.

God's statements in Genesis 1 are of the same ilk as prophecies because God is stating from Heaven what he will accomplish in the future on Earth. To this day, he has always achieved what he has foretold.

It is as we learn in Matthew 19:26, that "With God, all things are possible."

God expects humankind to view the wonder of fulfilled prophecy as a definite proof of his existence and control of events over Time, as can be seen from his words in Isaiah 46:9-11

> I am God and there is none like me. I make known the end *from the beginning*, from ancient times what is still to come. I say, "My *purpose* will stand, and I will do all that I please."

Notice how God's prophesied actions *from the beginning* line up with his long-term *purpose*. Prophecy is comparable to God's stated *purposes* planned in Genesis for the Creation—to happen in Time in our Cosmos—that have and still do come to pass.

> "Who, then, is like me? Let him proclaim it; let him declare... what is yet to come – yes, let them foretell what will come. Do not tremble, do not be afraid; did I not proclaim this and *foretell* it long ago? You are my witnesses. Is there any God besides me?" Isaiah 44:7,8

Christ's life, death and resurrection were described in minute detail in over a hundred biblical prophecies centuries before he lived on Earth. The odds against this being just good guesswork are astronomical and trillions of times beyond the figure that statisticians regard as "absurd".

No other religious leader has had God's detailed prophetic seal of approval and purpose on his life: not Mohammed, not Buddha, not Gandhi, not Confucius, not Zoroaster, not Baha'u'llah... nor anyone else in all history, religious leader or not. Some of these leaders are on historical record as very good people and were doing their best—but only Jesus is written about as God's planned personal pathway to forgiveness and acceptance.

It is significant that Jesus is the only founder of a religion that is regularly reported to meet with NDErs in the afterlife, and in hundreds of reports at that. This is usually a surprise to people of other faiths or none.

Secular writings tell us that even in his own day, Jesus was accepted as a prophet of God.

Jesus is also the only religious leader acknowledged in a spiritual capacity by all major religions to some degree. Jews ancient and modern typically accept that Jesus was a Rabbi and popular Teacher. Buddhists will say Jesus was a great Teacher, and the Dalai Lama lauded Jesus as the model of a "spiritually mature, good, and warm-hearted person." The home I visited of an ardent Hindu had a picture of Jesus displayed centrally over the mantelpiece. Our Hindu hostess explained "Jesus is my Master". Jesus (Isa) is mentioned directly 25 times and indirectly over 150 times in the Quran and Islam upholds him as a *great prophet*. Compare this to Mohammad who is only mentioned directly in the Quran a handful of times. Jesus is certainly unique in his mention in religious writings.

If Jesus is a prophet of God in different religions, we should at least consider very carefully what he prophesied for our planet and for our personal futures.

Now let's link Time, Prophecy and Creation in a further example of God fulfilling his prophetic declarations. Consider the observation "when the *set Time* had fully come, God sent his Son, born of a woman, born under the law" (Galatians 4:4).

Since God the Father had previously determined when he would send us his son, Jesus came at precisely that Time, when the world was ready for him. For example, 1Peter 1:20 teaches:

> He (Jesus) was chosen *before* the Creation of the world, but was revealed in these last times for your sake.

The choice of Jesus therefore preceded the Creation. This was a choice made in heavenly Time, before earthly Time began! Wow!

However, this is more than just a "Wow" factor. God reveals his planning because he wants us to recognise and respond to Jesus at a personal level.

Looking at the detailed fulfilment of prophecy should not leave the impression that personal responsibility is cancelled. For example, King Jeroboam was promised an enduring dynasty providing he kept God's decrees and commands as King David had (1Kings 11:38). He had the choice and failed—therefore his dynasty failed too.

God's dealings in our lives are similarly not all predetermined in detail. Outcomes depend at least partly on our choices, although we cannot know yet to what extent.

It is our reactions to life events that are most important. Our responses develop our character and relationship with God while we are still on Earth.

To God, our reactions are much more important than any actual events—and that includes sicknesses, failed relationships, family tragedies, business failures, becoming refugees, and other trials and tribulations.

We find this principle confirmed in scripture:

Romans 5:3,4 – "We also glory in our sufferings, because we know that suffering produces perseverance; perseverance, character; and character, hope."

James 1:2-4 – "Consider it pure joy, my brothers and sisters, whenever you face trials of many kinds, because you know that the testing of your faith produces perseverance. Let perseverance finish its work so that you may be mature and complete, not lacking anything."

Although so much of life comes down to personal choice, please be encouraged in that God has prepared in advance the facility to forgive and forget our mistakes. This was dealt with by Jesus' crucifixion.

Prophetic fulfilment reveals much about God and how he continues to achieve things on Earth, to this very day, including his progressive implementation of the Creation.

Let's look more deeply into the interlinking of Time, prophecy and God's purposes. This enables us to grasp who we *actually* are and our origins and destiny.

CHAPTER 5

DIGGING DEEPER INTO TIME AND PROPHECY

"I've read the last page of the Bible.
It's all going to turn out all right."

—Billy Graham[10]

The coming of Jesus split our classification of Time in the West neatly into two epochs—BC and AD.

To better appreciate who we are truly and our own future, we need to consider the Messiah, Jesus, who dominates both Old and New Testament scripture and was one with God the Father before the start of Creation.

Consider an important event that occurred soon after Jesus' crucifixion. Philip, a disciple of Jesus, was running beside the chariot of a very important official from Ethiopia when he heard the man reading aloud from the biblical book of Isaiah, chapter 53. We know that its prophecy pre-dated Christ's death because the book of Isaiah was written approximately seven centuries before those events in Jesus' life and death that are described in it so graphically, and we have a full copy of the book carbon-dated to around 125 BC.

As Philip ran beside the chariot, he spoke to the official (Acts 8:30-35):

"Do you understand what you are reading?" Philip asked.
"How can I," he said, "unless someone explains it to me?"
So, he invited Philip to come up and sit with him.
This is the passage of scripture the eunuch was reading:

> "He was led like a sheep to the slaughter,
> and as a lamb before its shearer is silent,
> so he did not open his mouth.
> In his humiliation he was deprived of justice.
> Who can speak of his descendants?
> For his life was taken from the Earth."

The eunuch asked Philip, "Tell me, please, who is the prophet talking about, himself or someone else?"

Then Philip began with that very passage of scripture and told him the good news about Jesus.

The good news which Philip told the important Ethiopian was that God's Saviour, described clearly in the Isaiah passage he was reading, had now come! That Saviour was Jesus of Nazareth, who had recently been executed by the Romans, but had risen from the grave to demonstrate to hundreds of witnesses that he held the keys to resurrection life.

The official believed him about Jesus, stopped his carriage and was baptised by Philip in some water nearby. The ancient Christian church of Ethiopia traces its origin back to this incident.

Of significance, Philip and the early church already recognised soon after the crucifixion that this ancient prophecy in Isaiah 53 put God's personal seal and signature on Jesus as the Messiah!

Their confidence was because God, in Heaven, in whatever time frame he works in there, had described in detail in Isaiah 53 an event that would happen only in the distant future on Earth, and the things they had witnessed for themselves absolutely identified this event to Philip, Peter, John and many others.

Now matters are about to become extraordinary.

Isaiah 53, which the Ethiopian was reading, describes the ministry and sufferings of Jesus in some detail and is quoted in other places of the New Testament, always in the *past tense* by scholars of that era and currently too, yet the events it described happened seven centuries *after* it was first written! How could the distant future be written about so precisely *in the past tense*?

This is highly significant in terms of Time and God's timing.

Isaiah 53 was originally written in biblical Hebrew, which is not a "tenses" language. The verb is generally seen as past or future, depending on context, and if it refers to the future it is called a prophetic perfect. Scholars, translators and commentators choose the past tense for an event, past NOT future, that is *absolutely definite and settled*. This is the past tense that was chosen for Isaiah 53.

This explanation applies to other descriptions from Isaiah 53, e.g. verse 5

> he *was* pierced for our transgressions,
> he *was* crushed for our iniquities;
> the punishment that brought us peace *was* on him,
> and by his wounds we are healed.

The earliest Greek translation of the Book of Isaiah in the Bible is found in the Septuagint, which derived its named from the belief that seventy of the best Jewish scholars supposedly conferred and conducted its translation from Hebrew into Greek long before Jesus was born. What is extraordinary is that the Greek language, unlike Hebrew, has strict past, present and future tenses—and these early pre-Christian Hebrew scholars chose to employ the precise *past tense* for Isaiah 53, despite the actual events only happening in what would be the distant future. They were very particular in applying the past tense in their translations.

Therefore, Isaiah 53 confirms that the crucifixion, and all that it means for our rescue from future punishment at Judgement, was already a "done deal" from God's point of view in Heaven, long before Christ's actual sacrifice took place on our planet. It was essentially a completed action from the moment God decided it in Heaven.

Similarly, the Creation was a completed plan when God decided it as described in Genesis 1. It has been implemented progressively ever since in our Universe, until today. The Creation will also continue into our future.

Something even more startling about Time and timings emerges as we look at the ministry of Christ in the New Testament.

Isaiah 53:6 reveals that it was on the cross that God "laid upon him the iniquity (sin) of us all"—the past tense showing again that it was a "done deal" in God's heavenly timing although it had not yet happened on Earth. This nevertheless confirmed that forgiveness for sins would come from Christ's substitutionary death on Earth.

Now things are about to get truly mind blowing—vital aspects of Jesus' ministry, *before he was actually crucified*, depended upon his personal sacrifice *that was still to happen on Earth!!* For example, he forgave sins (Matthew 9:2; Luke 7:48) and healed many people.

Matthew 8:16,17 confirms this extraordinary timing:

> When evening came, many who were demon-possessed were brought to him, and he drove out the spirits with a word and healed all the sick. *This was to fulfil what was spoken though the prophet Isaiah (Isaiah 53:4)—*
>
> > "He took up our infirmities
> > and bore our diseases".

Let's dwell on this extraordinary situation a little longer. Isaiah around 700 BC was foretelling the consequences resulting from the death of the future Messiah, that he would take our infirmities and diseases upon himself so that provision for these could be made for us. Matthew 8:17 is proclaiming that Jesus centuries later was *already* healing people on the basis of his own impending death, described in Isaiah and written down centuries earlier, but which had *not yet* happened on our planet! Despite this, Jesus was *already* forgiving sins and doing the healings that would be accomplished during his own future crucifixion on Earth.

How can we make sense of that?

We can only conclude that in one sense, Jesus' death had already happened from the perspective of God in Heaven because he had declared it—past tense. But for Jesus on Earth, the horror of the cross lay ahead—future tense.

This illustrates two stages of timing exist for earthly reality:

Stage 1 – God in Heaven credits an event to have happened already when he decides it in Heaven and scripture records it as such—in advance of it actually happening on Earth.

Stage 2 – Humankind on Earth experiences that event which God has already decided in Heaven, frequently after many earthly years. It may then happen in an instant, or as a development that takes a short or long time.

This also explains how Jesus was declared in 1Peter 1:20 to be "chosen *before* the Creation of the world, but was *revealed in these last times* for your sake". This is a crystal-clear statement of how Two-Stage Process works. Similarly, Revelation 13:8 identifies Jesus as the sacrificial lamb "who was slain from the Creation of the world".

Both of the above quotes were written in the Greek language in the New Testament, with its strict attention to the past and future.

A further unexpected feature of scripture arises from this principle:

> *God is purpose-focussed rather than Time-focussed, such that scripture may range widely and unexpectedly through Time on Earth.*

For example, when one of God's authors inspired by the Holy Spirit is writing about the Messiah in the Bible, the Holy Spirit is concerned for the mission of that special person and the details may span many centuries in a sentence. This is why the Jews of Jesus' day expected a coming King as well as a Saviour, all at the same time. They did not realise that many centuries would separate two comings. The first coming was the incarnation at Bethlehem, the second will be the "Second Coming" shortly before the Judgement.

The famous quote from Isaiah 9:6,7 illustrates this distinction:

> For to us a child is born, to us a son is given (*First Coming*), and the government will be on his shoulders (*Second Coming*).
>
> Of the greatness of his government and peace there will be no end. He will reign on David's throne and over his kingdom, establishing and upholding it with justice and righteousness from that Time on and forever (*Second Coming—continuing after Judgement*).

Between Christ's coming as a child, and his future return to the Earth to rule and reign, twenty centuries have elapsed already. However, one *purpose* of the child was to rule and reign at some future Time, and so this intention is confirmed within a few words of his prophesied first coming. The purpose remains unchanging while it is Time that flows.

> *Purpose, determined by God in Heaven, takes*
> *precedence over timing on Earth!*

This is a vital principle for us to remember in our own lives and plans. In fact, who we *truly* are, and why, is contingent upon God's purposes for us rather than on timing.

A comparable spanning of Time and timing being subservient to purpose was identified when Jesus personally selected a passage to read aloud in the

Nazareth synagogue. He unrolled the scroll, found Isaiah 61:1,2, then read aloud the ancient prophecy about himself (Luke 4:16-21):

> "The Spirit of the Lord is on me,
> because he has anointed me
> to proclaim good news to the poor.
> He has sent me to proclaim freedom for the prisoners
> and recovery of sight for the blind,
> to set the oppressed free,
> to proclaim the year of the Lord's favour."
>
> Then he rolled up the scroll, gave it back to the attendant and sat down. The eyes of everyone in the synagogue were fastened on him.
> He began by saying to them, "***Today*** this scripture is fulfilled in your hearing."

Note that the anointing and the authority to do these things had not been given at Jesus' birth, or at his baptism some weeks before when the Holy Spirit descended upon him, or during his encounter with Satan in the wilderness, or even the previous day—it was only fulfilled *that very day* on which he announced the start of his public ministry.

But why did Jesus stop reading the scroll there? It is because the verse in Isaiah continued with the phrase, "...and the day of vengeance of our God", and Jesus was not ready to proclaim that, because it was not yet God's Time for that to happen. Until now, that day still lies ahead.

Prophecies can catch us by surprise, in the sense that predicted events which we expect to happen in a slow development can do so with unanticipated rapidity. For example, twenty-five forecasted details from the Old Testament of Christ's betrayal, trial, death and burial were fulfilled within only twenty-four hours at the end of his life. I wonder how many of these were recognised by the learned spiritual leaders of the day? Some of these leaders had even been complicit in his judicial murder, despite the ringing prophecies describing his suffering and death. The Apostle Paul in 1Corinthians 2:7-8 gives an insightful explanation that in addition confirms the accuracy of prophecy beginning in Heaven but spanning many centuries on Earth:

> We declare God's wisdom, a mystery that has been hidden
> and that God destined for our glory *before time began.*
> None of the rulers of this age understood it, for if they
> had, they would not have crucified the Lord of glory.

What does "Time in Heaven" involve, where important events on Earth are predetermined, and why has God designed humankind to function on a planet in a Universe that is characterised by a different Time and timings to those in Heaven?

Let's explore this question that is especially relevant to the Creation—and to ourselves personally.

CHAPTER 6

TIME IN HEAVEN

"And surely I am with you always, to the very end of the age"
(Matthew 28:20)

—Jesus Christ

Time, for God in Heaven, plainly does not follow the same rules as Time does for us on Earth.

One of the primary blocks to our comprehending scripture is forgetting—or not realising—that Heaven is *not* timeless; although Time likely passes differently there to Time in our world.

Our experience of Time on Earth is preparing us for the afterlife.

Let's begin with some statements made by Jesus.

Shortly before his crucifixion, Jesus prayed aloud (John 17:5):

"And now, Father, glorify me in your presence with the glory I had with you *before* the world began".

Jesus is pointing out there was Time in Heaven before the Creation of our world.

Prior to the Earth's Creation, Jesus shared the glory of God the Father. In the verse above, he asked to return to be with the Father in Heaven.

He came from Heaven and remained in contact with God the Father there, and consequently speaks with authority on the subject. His words were recorded in the New Testament in the Greek language. I will italicise future tenses in the quote below to draw attention to them:

> Matthew 8:11,12 – "I say to you that many *will come* from the east and the west, and *will take* their places at the feast with Abraham, Isaac and Jacob in the Kingdom of Heaven. But the subjects of the Kingdom *will be* thrown outside, into the darkness, where there *will be* weeping and gnashing of teeth".

Since Jesus was able to describe future events within the Kingdom of Heaven, it must operate with a future not only from our perspective, but within its own framework.

Here is a reference Jesus made to God's house in Heaven, where God dwells:

> John 14:2,3 – "My Father's house has many rooms (the accurate translation is not "mansions"); if that were not so, would I have told you that I am going there to prepare a place for you? And if I go and prepare a place for you, I will come back and take you to be with me, that you also may be where I am".

Time must be passing for Jesus in Heaven if he goes there at one specific time and then returns at another. Besides, Jesus states that he *will* prepare a place in Heaven for his disciples, an activity in the future that would require an input of time. Jesus is not inactive in Heaven right now; he is serving in a sanctuary there (Hebrews 8:2) and interceding (praying) for us (Romans 8:34). All these actions require a framework of heavenly Time.

There are other activities described in scripture as taking place in Heaven. In the past there was rebellion and war. There is the holding of court, discussion, rejoicing, creating, active worshipping, talking. Each of these by nature involves the passing of time. Heaven is not a timeless warp, as some conjecture.

Those in Heaven are aware of the passage of Time there. Revelation 6:10 describes the martyrs: "They called out in a loud voice, 'How long, Sovereign Lord, holy and true, until you judge the inhabitants of the Earth and avenge our blood?'" Without a doubt, *how long* is time-related. Verse 11 continues: "Then each of them was given a white robe, and they were told to *wait a little longer...*"

Therefore, there is no sensible biblical basis for doubting that Time exists right now in Heaven.

Time in Heaven displays comforting similarities to Time on Earth.

What might the Time spans be called in Heaven? On Earth we have hours, days, weeks and months etc, but what might they have in Heaven?

Heaven certainly has "hours":

> "There was silence in Heaven for about *half an hour*" (Revelation 8:1).

Scripture also teaches us that both "day" and "night" are descriptors used in and about Heaven.

> *In Matthew 26:29, Jesus commented on the wine he and his disciples were drinking at their last meal together; "I tell you, I will not drink from this fruit of the vine (wine) from now on until *that day* when I drink it new with you in My Father's Kingdom". Not only is Jesus pinpointing a future event to be shared with his disciples, but describes it as occurring at a unit of Time called a "day".

> *The Book of Revelation gives us some of our best illumination of Heaven. It was written by the Apostle John, who was taken on a visit

to Heaven in the first century, and who described what he saw there. In Revelation 4:8 John tells us that *"day and night* they never stop saying 'Holy, holy, holy is the Lord God Almighty, who was, and is, and is to come'".

Time, and how it passes, is pivotally important to us humans; it shapes how we plan and perceive things.

Heaven, where God is domiciled, existed before the world was formed. Since we carry God's image, we should function best in an environment with certain chosen similarities to Heaven.

> *Our **days** in this world are thereby preparing us*
> *for living within heavenly **days** later.*

It is helpful while studying scripture to keep in mind that Heaven today will be different to the New Heaven of the future. Heaven at any point in Time is God's dwelling place. Consider Apostle John's vision of the future "New Heaven" described in Revelation 21: 1-3

> Then I saw "a New Heaven and a New Earth," for the first Heaven and the first Earth had passed away, and there was no longer any sea. I saw the Holy City, the New Jerusalem, coming down out of Heaven from God, prepared as a bride beautifully dressed for her husband. And I heard a loud voice from the throne saying, "Look! God's *dwelling place is now among the people, and he will dwell with them.* They will be his people, and God himself will be with them and be their God.

In Revelation 21:22-25 it teaches that in the future New Heaven, in a wonderful city called the New Jerusalem that will come down from the present Heaven, and in a fresh Cosmos identified as the New Heavens, there will be no need for the sun because instead God will supply its light.

Please always remember that Heaven today is different to what the New Heaven will be like in the distant future—after Judgement.

Even in the idyllic conditions that will exist in the New Jerusalem after Judgement, there will be the passing of Time—despite there being no need for a sun to shine, because God the Father and Jesus will supply all the light needed.. Consider Revelation 22:2, "On each side of the river stood the tree of life, bearing twelve crops of fruit, yielding its fruit *every month*". This shows that this stupendous city of the future will operate with "months"—this should help us adapt to being there. Perhaps there will be twelve-month years there similar to ours on our planet? Perhaps. Certainly, Time and its measurement will continue.

Nevertheless, the measurement of Time in Heaven nowadays. and other afterlife locations in the future, may not be related to a sun or to light or dark, even if the use of terms such as "day" and "night" may be retained for measuring Time—perhaps retained because these terms could give us comfort in that we understand them?

The continuing use of corresponding terminology for the passing of Time in every age and Venue to come in the afterlife is a further example of God's love, who makes plans for us that we can anticipate even now with the expectation that we will belong and feel "at home". This feeling of being "at home" in the afterlife is very commonly reported by NDErs, often to their great surprise and even wonderment.

In addition, we are promised (1Corinthians 15:53,54) that we will eventually have immortal physical bodies, and there are certain heart-warming and interesting activities described in Heaven that we will enjoy. Activities require Time.

The existence of Time in Heaven nowadays enables it to be an active and vibrant place.

The Bible retains a number of descriptive terms about Heaven that are readily understood from our lives on Earth, such as "speaking", "singing", "drinking", "rooms", "rivers", "glass", "light", "feasting", "throwing out", "worshipping", and much besides.

What does God do during his days in Heaven this side of Judgement Day? Many things. One important activity mentioned in scripture is that he has held court, most likely of supernatural beings including angels, and perhaps continues to do so.

Let's consider the description of these sessions of court in Heaven. In Job 1:6 we find a significant detail mentioned:

> "One *day* the angels came to present themselves before the Lord, and Satan also came with them…"

And in Job 2:1,2:

> On another *day*, the angels came to present themselves before the Lord, and Satan also came with them to present himself before him.
> And the Lord said to Satan, "Where have you come from?"
> Satan answered the LORD, "From roaming throughout the Earth, going back and forth on it."

Other events have similarly been described as happening in Heaven during days there, in particular the days of Creation in Genesis 1.

Let's ponder those days of Creation that took place in Heaven.

Some Bible scholars would prefer the "days" described in Genesis 1 to take place somewhere on or near Earth rather than in Heaven. But our sun marks out our days for us on Earth. How, then, could our sun be created only on Day 4 of Creation and not Day 1—how had the first three days of Creation been marked out on Earth before the sun had been created to mark out those days?

God's clear and stated purpose for creating the stars, sun and moon, which he did on the 4th day, was to mark out on Earth "seasons and ***days*** and years." (Genesis 1:14–19)

This is not a contradiction nor an issue for believers who see Genesis 1 as describing God planning his Creation of the Universe, within and from Heaven, during those six heavenly days.

Some Creationists calculating God's activity in Heaven incorrectly by Earth days go to great lengths and imagination to reconcile God's delay in creating the sun with their different interpretations of the six Creation days. However, all end up with an unconvincing proposal, as well as dismissing God's stated plan for the demarcation of the days.

Trying to conceptualise the order of events in Genesis 1, other than as a Heaven based blue-print for unfolding Creation on our planet later on, becomes mind-boggling and unbelievable. As an example, on Day 3 the land was producing vegetation and trees bearing fruit already, all without the sunlight that only began on Day 4. But photosynthesis for the plants, trees and fruit requires the sun.

Time and seasons on Earth are still acknowledged today as depending on celestial movements and measurements, as God designed to be the case during Day 4 in Heaven. Even the Universal Time measurements, that we have developed to such phenomenal accuracy, depend on the movement of celestial bodies relative to the Earth.

Days on Earth are marked out by the sun, whether or not we realise that this was decreed by God. Quite how days in Heaven are marked out, we don't yet know.

My discussions that follow assume that all the creative activity in Genesis 1 from Day 1 to Day 7 occurred entirely in Heaven, during heavenly days, and that the Cosmos, including our planet and life forms on it, have materialised at different times after these heavenly activities.

God in Heaven can speak of things that are not yet on Earth—as though they were. Romans 4:17 in the amplified Bible reinforces this concept in its expanded language, saying that God "speaks of the non-existent things that [He has foretold and promised] as if they [already] existed." This is precisely what he was doing in Genesis 1.

Statements such as "God saw that it was good," in verses 4,10,12, 18, 24 fit this. And the summary in the last verse of Genesis 1 – verse 31 – was that "God saw all that he had made, and it was very good" does not mean that they were already finished products in our Universe. Instead, it denotes that God envisioned and planned them to be made in the Universe he was designing, and he was pleased with the plans he had made.

Seeing the "days" of Creation (Genesis 1–Genesis 2.3) as days of creating in Heaven, where God lives and plans, to be implemented subsequently in our Universe, enables us to appreciate the processes of God's innovative genius, a God who continues to create to this very day.

Scripture indicates that Time may not proceed at the same rate in Heaven as on Earth. It may pass more slowly in Heaven so that our lives and events can be viewed from there rather like a toy that has been wound up and revolves very fast. If so, both Earth and Heaven would have Time future, Time present and Time past, but we would be arriving at them at different rates.

We don't yet know the correlation of earthly Time to heavenly Time, but I agree in essence with Pastor [11] Todd Burpo:

> It was also possible that Time in Heaven doesn't track with Time on Earth.
>
> The Bible says that with the Lord, "a day is like a thousand years, and a thousand years are like a day" (2Peter 3:8). Some interpret that as a literal exchange, as in, two days equals two thousand years. I've always taken it to mean that God operates outside of our understanding of time.

Absolutely.

The main point is that God, as the architect of both Heaven and the Universe, can change and adjust the passage of Time in either location as he chooses—such that a day in Heaven could correspond to the passing of vast amounts of Time on Earth, and vice versa, as he might decide.

I think it likely that the Universe began to be constructed consecutively only after the completion of God's planning it in six heavenly days and God's subsequent day of rest. Using key scriptures, I will explain further along in this book why I favour this model above all others.

Physicists assure us that, even within our Cosmos, Time passes at different rates in different locations. On realising this, a plethora of new and fascinating possibilities opens up.

While writing this chapter, I read that Stephen Hawking had died. Hawking was arguably the most influential Scientist in modern times and we will be the poorer for his passing. I also learnt that shortly before he died, he had reversed his earlier stand that Time itself began at the inception of the Universe. Unfortunately, he had already promoted his earlier theory in numerous writings, lectures and interviews.

Many Bible-believing Christians always knew that Hawking was wrong on this issue—Time of some sort existed outside the Universe long before our Cosmos was created. Consequently, Hawking's ultimate concept of a different sort of Time in a different dimension pre-existing the appearance of the Universe is quite scriptural.

Hawking has left a colossal challenge for today's youth, released posthumously, to "Wonder about what makes the world exist". It is absolutely vital for us all, not simply the youth, to embark upon that quest.

I wonder whether Physicists will begin recognising as deriving from outside our Cosmos those elegant equations that describe the forces that determine its fundamental functioning and structure?

From there it could be a small step for mainstream Science to decide that the Universe must have been designed and could not have been the product of blind forces.

Please excuse my silly pun, but I have to say it or I'll burst—"Time will tell"!

PART 3

YOUR TIME

IN THE AFTERLIFE

CHAPTER 7

NDEs, Shadow Theory, and Transfer Principle

"For now we see through a glass darkly…" (1 Corinthians 13:12a KJV)

—Apostle Paul

How do you experience Time on Earth, and how will you experience Time differently when you die and pass into the afterlife?

Thousands of reports from NDErs help us see more clearly answers to these interlinked questions, and so does scripture.

I propose two principles to facilitate our understanding of Time both in this life and that to come. One I have called Shadow Theory, which I will describe before leading into the second, the Transfer Principle. They share similarities except that while Shadow Theory functions for us during life on Earth, the Transfer Principle functions after death, during a Near Death Experience and beyond.

———•※•———

Heaven existed first before our solar system. In certain respects, Earth copies or "shadows" *pre-existing* realities found in Heaven.

Genesis 1:26 reads "Then God said, 'Let us make mankind in our image, in our likeness'. The word translated "image" carries in biblical Hebrew the root picture of "a shadow" of God. Is there a deep purpose at work here?

There certainly is. At our best, mankind only projects a shadow of who God is in Heaven.

One problem with shadows generally is that they provide an indistinct, flat 2D resemblance of a 3D object or scene in full colour. The shadow of a friend carries his outline and may even allow you to recognise him, but is dull compared with a face-to-face encounter. Likewise, the "shadows" of God and his Heaven that we may conceptualise on Earth lack their true brilliance and depth. We cannot even imagine their splendour. The Apostle Paul confirmed this when writing his first letter of advice to the Corinthian church (1Corinthians 2:9):

> As it is written (Isaiah 64:4):
>
> "What no eye has seen,
> what no ear has heard,
> and what no human mind has conceived
> are the things God has prepared for those who love him."

This process of thought became what I have called "Shadow Theory". It has helped me to comprehend better the relationship between Heaven and Earth, and how and why God creates things.

Simply expressed, Shadow Theory states that it is because we are made in the image and likeness of God, that the world is designed to be like Heaven in the first place, but only in certain simplified respects.

To express this similarity, the Bible employs the words "copy", "image" and "shadow". All three words mean different things but all are a "representation of something real", and I am using the term Shadow Theory as a composite to encompass them all. The verses below illustrate this principle:

> Hebrews 10:1, "The Law is only a *shadow* of the good things that are coming—not the realities themselves".

Colossians 2:16,17, "Do not let anyone judge you by what you eat or drink, or with regard to a religious festival, a New Moon celebration or a Sabbath day. These are a *shadow* of the things to come, the reality is found in Christ".

Hebrews 8:5, "They serve at a sanctuary that is a *copy* and *shadow* of what is in Heaven".

Hebrews 9:24, "For Christ did not enter a man-made sanctuary that was only a *copy* of the true one, he entered Heaven itself, now to appear for us in God's presence".

Each of the earthly things above is a *shadow* or *copy* of something *already in existence* in Heaven.

The Greek word translated as "shadow" carries the perception of a "rough sketch". It was used of an artist who produced preliminary sketches on which his final composition was developed. The sketches in Leonardo da Vinci's notebooks, while very good, pale beside his final masterpieces.

Shadow Theory underlines that we must never make the mistake of according life on Earth too much importance. The design and formation of our world is just a part of a higher plan, and we should see it as simply another piece in a stunning jigsaw, or a further thread in a beautiful tapestry. Otherwise it becomes impossible to perceive our lives in context, or even to explore more precisely than before the underpinning nature of God.

Shadow Theory highlights fundamental similarities between humans and Father God, producing helpful links in our comprehension of Earth and Heaven. These "shadows" enable lessons learnt here to transfer into our future. Similar lessons will continue after Judgement and into the New Heaven and New Earth.

GOD'S CREATIVITY AND NEAR DEATH EXPERIENCES

Why are we considering NDEs in a book about our origins and who we truly are? This is a valid question.

Very simply, NDEs provide extraordinary insight into God's resourceful genius by considering some of the features of the other places God has created besides our Earth and our Universe. These features help us to unravel a little regarding the deeper nature of Time, Love, Energy and Consciousness. Life on our planet, amazing though it is, does not go far enough to unpack these mysteries in any depth. We can ponder them using the reports of returnees, who assure us that each is experienced somewhat differently in the afterlife.

Modern resuscitation techniques and their success, allied to the availability of the Internet, have given rise to people reporting temporary afterlife experiences far more often than ever before in history. The similarities between their thousands of written accounts gives confidence that NDEs can augment not detract from our perception and appreciation of God's ingenuity. Personally, I have found the subject so interesting over five decades that I have researched it extensively, and written on it comprehensively in my last book *Living Beyond—Making Sense of Near Death Experiences*.

The NDE begins when a person's spirit (consciousness) floats up and out of the body and generally can see its lifeless body below. Some NDErs return quickly to their bodies and earthly life resumes, but the spirits of others proceed to new adventures in the afterlife. These occur mainly in a location for spirits termed Hades in the Bible—which predominantly comprises pleasant rural or garden sections called Paradise, as well as unpleasant Prison sections. The walls and buildings of God's Heavenly City can often be seen in the distance from Paradise.

Many NDErs meet with God the Father or with Jesus in remarkable locations, usually in Paradise sections but sometimes in Prison ones, or more rarely within the Heavenly City itself, before returning to their bodies on Earth—often suddenly.

A significant number of these NDE reports are by Doctors and Scientists of one discipline or another, who have been trained to provide exact observations of what they have experienced. Their descriptions glove together impressively.

The remarkable gardens and countrified surroundings of the Heavenly City are a part of the Paradise to which Jesus took the thief who died on the cross beside him, having reassured him already that "TODAY you will be with me in Paradise" (Luke 23:43). Notice that he was to be with Jesus in Paradise that day—where departed human spirits wait for Judgement Day—and not the Heavenly City, also called "Heaven", where God lives.

We know that Jesus' body remained behind for burial while his spirit went to Hades, and not yet to God the Father in Heaven, so his promise to the thief must have been for them both to travel to the Paradise section of Hades.

Please note that NDEs do not happen in Heaven as a rule, but in the sections of Paradise or the Prisons in Hades. Heaven, or Hell, become destinations only after final Judgement has taken place sometime in the future.

Thousands of NDErs describe Paradise nowadays as astoundingly gorgeous; it displays the artistic side of God to us at a new and previously undreamt-of intensity. Here is a recent description by [12] Barbara D of her NDE: which she had at age 13 years, but only written down by Barbara more recently:

> I first looked for the sun but found nothing that provided a light source for the daylight conditions.
>
> I then looked across the river, to see such an amazing world of mountains, trees, waterfalls, exotic flowers. Everywhere was green, green, green! It looked like our own natural world, but on steroids.
>
> There was so much life with colors, textures, light, and smells that were all in a state of absolute perfection and abundance. I could scarcely take it in.

GOD'S CREATIVITY AND THE TRANSFER PRINCIPLE

A startling fact emerges as we study NDEs:

> *Afterlife Venues share many common characteristics with our world.*

These Venues are designed by God so that while they are very different in certain respects, there remain sufficient "tags" or similarities to our lives that we are not totally disoriented or even fearful as our spirit moves into these new realities.

In short, familiar features enable people to *transfer* smoothly into afterlife places and subsequently between them, and settle quickly into the new Venues—I term this process "the Transfer Principle".

The Transfer Principle states formally that "conditions on Earth share similarities to conditions in afterlife Venues, devised by a loving God to facilitate our functioning successfully there."

Five notable examples of this principle would be Time, consciousness, communication, relationships and light. Very briefly:

> Regarding *Time*—NDErs in the main notice that Time exists in all afterlife Venues, including Heaven and Hades, but they say that it appears to pass differently from Time on Earth. Nevertheless, because we are familiar with Time passing on Earth, at death our transfer from this world to afterlife Time appears not to be daunting.
>
> Regarding *consciousness*—NDErs say we remain ourselves and fully conscious of our existence, even though we have died! Fear usually disappears, and pain always does so immediately at death.
>
> Regarding *communication*—thousands of written records by NDErs without exception recount how communication in the afterlife was by telepathy. Since this telepathy conveyed comprehensive, earthly knowledge and concepts, they adapted to it quickly and responded in kind. Nevertheless, it was extraordinary as a means of communication because thoughts and emotions were laid bare and could not be hidden, such as we often do when we associate with one another on our planet.
>
> Regarding *relationships*—NDErs discover *love* continues after death and appears to be the coinage of relationships in the afterlife. They generally meet joyfully with parents and other family members who had pre-deceased them, including ancestors whom they had not known previously.

Regarding *light*—Paradise and the Heavenly City are suffused in a brilliant light, similar but superior to light in our world because it connects directly into the soul—for example feelings of love, compassion and acceptance seem conveyed through it to the NDEr. New arrivals find it welcoming and comforting. Fiona M[13] recently described it in these words: "I did experience a most exquisite light. It was not hard to the eyes and it was a very special light unlike what we see here on Earth. It was vastly peaceful and gracious. The peacefulness is what I remember most."

However, light has not been experienced in the same way for those unfortunate NDErs who have been relegated to one of the Prison sections of Hades. These are characterised by dim lighting or, in the case of the Void, little or no lighting at all.

These similarities to Earth involving Time, consciousness, communication, relationships and light facilitate the NDEr absorbing the important fresh lessons that have been prepared for them in the afterlife.

Prevalence of NDEs

Most NDErs are initially hesitant to speak about what happened to them. There are various reasons for this: concerns expressed by family or friends are common, as are social and professional reasons, and even rejection by their religions. Nevertheless, more and more NDErs are giving their accounts—the NDERF website for example has copied more than 4500 first-hand descriptions that are available to us over the internet. While there are obvious individual differences, returnees from the afterlife nevertheless record startling similarities in their descriptions.

> *After lengthy consideration over many years I have concluded that each NDE was planned ingeniously by God as a learning experience for that particular returnee.*

Thereby, NDEs illustrate intriguing facets of God's ingenuity, including details of how he treats and cares for us individually.

What are we to make about the views of some who have experienced clinical death and revival with nothing to report about the interim? [14]Kerry Packer, the richest man in Australia at the time, had a heart attack in 1990 and was clinically dead for several minutes. Afterwards he would famously and emphatically tell those around him that there was "nothing out there".

Remembering that researchers have found that conservatively speaking only around one in ten who die and return to life report having had an NDE, or at least one that they remember—might we suggest that Kerry Packer was not in that group? For a gambler, he would surely have understood those odds.

NDEs—Beneficial or Not?

Looking at the effect on those who have had them, NDEs seem to be a divine gift from which to benefit. Many agnostics, atheists, Muslims, Christians, Hindus etc have found them to be life-changing, for the better. Follow-up studies conducted over some years have confirmed this.

Sadly, though, some returnees seem quite disorientated as they continue their lives, and become emotionally tangled. Too often they suffer rejection from family, friends, work colleagues, church leadership or congregations—resulting in stress and depression. They may suffer trauma similar to PTSD; some even resort to suicide. I know of such tragic cases. Others who have returned after suicide attempts, such as Angie Fenimore, generally report unpleasant afterlife experiences best avoided.

In some instances, the NDE may be primarily for the sake of others who will be helped by the transformed NDEr; a common example being mothers who return for the benefit of their children.

But unless God tells a particular NDEr the specific reasons for their return to the world, as a significant number have claimed has happened to them, we can only conjecture—because it is God alone who determines who will and who won't be granted an NDE, and for what purposes.

Accepting Insights Gained From NDEs

Here is a question to ponder: why have many people who would have not expected an afterlife experience or an encounter with God, returned to our world assuring us that they have had both, to their own amazement? What could have so radically changed their belief and their subsequent behaviour—some unanticipated hallucination maybe? This possibility has been discounted as ludicrous by Psychiatrists and Psychologists, some of whom have themselves experienced an NDE.

Might we expect Scientists to come up with something more objective and convincing regarding the afterlife than reports by revived patients?

They have.

The AWARE study is international, longitudinal and statistically relevant, led by highly regarded critical-care Physician Sam Parnia. He leads a multidisciplinary collaboration of international Scientists and Physicians conducting AWARE across many hospitals. It involves a clinical investigation of the brain and consciousness during cardiac arrest, including testing the validity of perceptions during the out-of-body part of near death experiences.

AWARE published some interim findings in August 2016.

Their analysis of the data available to that August led them to declare that **consciousness survives clinical death**, and logically must be independent of the brain, which is left behind in the lifeless body.

> *At last Scientists can accept (even if some refuse to,*
> *and some do so tentatively) that death may not be*
> *the end, and still remain true to Science!*

The way Science works, many further experiments must be devised and conducted before a definite scientific conclusion can be declared. This experimentation is growing apace.

Science and Medicine in all disciplines will never be quite the same again once Parnia's findings have been verified independently, as they surely will be in time. There is a massive amount of confirmatory material, including thousands of written accounts, to investigate and quantify, and it all points in the same direction.

Robert Lanza[15], voted in the New York Times as the third most important Scientist alive, supports absolutely that consciousness is not seated in the brain and that it survives physical death.

Once the continuation of consciousness is generally accepted, not only Science and Medicine, but Religion and humankind's approach to life itself will be transformed, sending us on a pursuit to uncover the meaning of our individual lives. Some readers of this book will already be on this personal quest—please keep going!

Hopefully, generations to come may begin living with eternity in mind rather than chasing the dirty dollar and personal comforts.

One would anticipate them to be thoughtful about their lives and God—and to spend their sojourn on the planet productively living lives characterised by love, service, and involvement in community activities.

ATHEISTS AND NDEs

Some of the confusion experienced in the accounts of atheists who have died may strike us as amusing, because they did not believe their consciousness would survive death, yet suddenly here they are in this new reality, and they must deal with it as best they can! Many, but not all, report initial experiences in a dimly lit Prison section.

During their afterlife experiences, some atheists reported being drawn towards a brilliant light, like moths drawn to a flame. Most who have approached near enough were startled to see the figure of a man from whom the light was streaming. Instinctively, they have identified this figure as God, God the Creator, or Jesus.

It appears that atheism may be an unnatural overlay that dissolves immediately one comes into God's presence—at which point some intuitive, possibly primeval, recognition kicks in.

No returnees from an NDE during which they met God are reported to remain disbelievers—confirmed amongst others by the findings of the researcher and prominent cardiologist Maurice Rawlings[16]. Rawlings, himself an erstwhile atheist, noted that every atheist NDEr he had interviewed had changed their viewpoint. It would be ridiculous to remain a sceptic after meeting and interacting with God. Rawlings investigated NDEs over some years and wrote extensively on his findings.

A number of atheists have become very effective Christian Ministers on return from their NDE. After all, they now *know* what agnostics may wonder about and atheists refute—that God is absolutely real, the source of existence, the brilliant consciousness from whose genius our Universe and ourselves derived. Prominent "atheists-subsequently-Ministers" include Howard Storm, Dr George Rodonaia, BJ McKelvie, Tim LaFond, and the "Box Jellyfish Man" Ian McCormack.

These former nonbelievers can become emotional when talking about meeting God in the afterlife: I remember Ian McCormack tearing up when telling us how compassionate and loving God was to him despite the dissolute life he had lived previously.

This discovery, even by atheists, that God appears to us as a compassionate man and not as some remote power has profound implications. One of these is that we can look forward to living where God lives, because we are more like him than we might ever have anticipated or imagined.

Church Ministry to NDErs

As for the increasing numbers of returning NDErs looking for new spiritual understanding and sympathy, will the Christian church worldwide rise up to meet this challenge, or will it leave them to the embrace of the New Age or other belief systems that already welcome NDErs warmly into their midst?

A Christian Doctor friend says that in her opinion the symptoms of disturbed returnees are very similar to PTSD. Many need love and counsel desperately, but instead feel rejected like lepers by their church families.

The first step would be for churches themselves to learn about NDErs, and to welcome them into their congregations, rather than driving them into other religions—as happens all too frequently nowadays.

All Christian denominations should aim to provide teaching materials and lectures for their Ministers, trainee Ministers, and congregations on what actually happens after death.

I received an email recently from an esteemed Professor in an American seminary who has attained several doctorates in different branches of theology. He had just read my last book "Living Beyond: Making Sense of Near Death Experiences". He wrote that he has never once seen advertised a Christian lecture to be presented in a seminary on the topic of what to anticipate on dying. Consequently, when he died, he was absolutely surprised by the NDE that followed! He now knows why so many NDErs give up on their churches; it is because they feel let down, believing that their church should have prepared them for what happens at death. Instead, they sense disbelief and even rejection from ignorant Ministers and congregations.

This same Professor, despite currently lecturing in an American seminary, admits that he cannot share his own experiences of the afterlife with his academic colleagues because they would criticise and perhaps reject what he would tell them. It is when he preaches away from his city in rural churches and mentions his NDE that "I get my only fellowship with those who themselves have had an NDE, who invariably stay behind and want to talk with me." Many express great relief that he knows what they are talking about, because he has been there himself.

Too many confused and even traumatised NDErs need answers and support after what has happened to them. They need acceptance, assistance, love and counsel from church leaders and other Christians. Otherwise, usually without saying anything, most will simply slip away. A significant amount of research has uncovered this alarming trend. This is despite many returnees claiming to be "more spiritually minded" following their NDE, but tragically finding that they can no longer trust the teachings found in their churches.

WAKE UP SEMINARIES! WAKE UP CHURCHES! Develop and preach a valid understanding of the afterlife to prepare your people and to help your NDErs!

NDEs Reveal God's Other Creations

Perhaps the biggest single revelation from NDEs is that God has created other Venues outside our Universe, and conceivably further Universes. These other places reported by NDErs who have been there are essentially different from ours, although sharing some likenesses—as will the coming New Heaven and the New Earth described in the Bible.

Secondly, the nature of existence in these other locations, including in Hades with its different levels in Paradise and Prison sections, is complex and different to that we enjoy on Earth.

On studying these afterlife locations as described by returnees, we conclude that God is by nature inventive, being not at all limited to the boundaries he has imposed on our Cosmos, nor to the relatively simple but elegant laws and principles that determine its functioning.

God is involved outside our Universe in creating what may even be a multiverse; detailed reliable descriptions of precisely what he is doing and how are not on record. Nevertheless, a number of reliable NDErs have been fortunate enough to be taken on tours hosted by angels, or more rarely by Jesus Christ. These tours occasionally included other Universes. Certain massive constructions and physical phenomena are described that are startling and unlike anything observed in ours, suggesting to the more scientific among NDErs that Laws of Physics new to us are involved.

Some returnees with scientific training have concluded that there is at least one extra spatial dimension in God's afterlife Venues, which makes descriptions of what is seen particularly difficult. Our descriptions have been composed for a 3D world and not a 4D one (or worlds having even more spatial dimensions); consequently, how to describe what happens there is evolving only slowly. And incidentally, if God has made a 4D Venue, he must occupy at least four dimensions himself—you cannot create in more dimensions than you live in yourself, can you?

God's ingenuity exhibits both his artistic brilliance and his scientific nature way beyond our imaginings. Why might he design and generate different Universes? We can only guess. Perhaps our own world can provide us with clues, but no more than that. Complex landscapes on Earth, for example under the sea where people have not been observers, or of previous life forms before humans even appeared on the planet, suggest he might take pleasure both in his artistry and in the myriad of interesting interactions within his Creations.

Both God the Father and Jesus have been described as displaying apparent pride at the beauties of their Paradise to newly arrived NDErs, who had expressed astonishment at the magnificence of what they were seeing.

NDEs, God and Time in the Afterlife

NDE reports are very revealing regarding Time in the afterlife.

Although most adult NDErs record experiences outside the Heavenly City, those few who have described entering it as short-term guests did not notice any accompanying change in the nature of Time, so it is likely that Time in the afterlife is alike both inside and outside the walls of the Heavenly City, although different to Time in our Universe.

Most returnees are confused when asked to explain what Time was like in whichever afterlife location they found themselves. They know that somehow its passing was not the same as on Earth, but in the main they cannot define the difference.

At death, our watches and mobile phones are left behind while it is our spirits in spirit bodies that have flown away. NDErs are consequently without their usual reference points respecting Time.

One of the reasons for their confusion is that experiences crowd in on the NDEr much more quickly than on our planet, where actions and comprehension are laborious in comparison. The transmission of information and conversation telepathically is also very rapid, and so is "seeing" the events of one's life during the Life Review.

One further difference between Time in Heaven and on Earth is relevant. On Earth, we are used to perceiving things sequentially because our eyes and our brains are interconnected. In the afterlife, our ponderous brains and neural systems have been left behind, and so multiple images and information can be absorbed by our souls all in the same moment.

Timing and Purpose of Return

On occasion, God provides a little information about their future to an NDEr before their return to the world. I have pondered the possible significance of this. Some instances strike me as parallel to Genesis 1, or specific biblical prophecies, where God stated in Heaven a sequence of what was going to happen on Earth—and it did—in subsequent earthly Time.

The experiences of many returnees illustrate that ultimately each of our lives rest more in God's hands than we are perhaps comfortable with. God often tells NDErs that they must return to our world because "your Time is not yet".

This truth appears in many scriptures such as the declaration of Psalm 31:15 that "My Times are in your hands".

An NDE is a sublime gift because it facilitates a course-correction for that NDEr on return to life. But very few in Paradise wish to take up an offer to return to Earth at all, because they are enjoying the afterlife very much and feel loved there.

To love more on return is the paramount lesson they report from their experiences. Why is this crucial?

The Bible actually reveals God's fundamental nature, that "God *is* Love" (1John 4:8). Therefore, loving people in all their complex variety helps us to "put the jigsaw together" and to know and love God more closely. Consequently, loving others is part of the general "mission" given to all humankind, not only to NDErs and not only to Christians.

It is not surprising, then, that literally thousands of NDErs have returned knowing that God has instructed them to practise love toward others, but few have comprehended at a deep level why this mission is quite so vital—that God *is* Love.

Many debates on spiritual topics, including the Creation/Evolution debate, hinge on when and where events were assumed to have taken place.

Too regularly, we suppose certain actions to apply only within our Universe and understanding, consequently taking no account of the proceedings and timings in Heaven.

I believe my Two-Stage Theory invites a whole new approach to comprehending how God does things, from Genesis to Revelation. So let's now apply it in more detail.

CHAPTER 8

TWO-STAGE THEORY AND GOD'S CREATIVITY

History is a vision of God's Creation on the move.

Arnold J. Toynbee[17]

When does a significant event actually happen?

This is not a silly question and the answer is not at all obvious. In fact, it's a challenging and pivotal question—our very existence remains uncertain and mysterious until we comprehend both the question and its answer:

> **Stage 1***: – **it happens in Heaven** when God first decrees, designs and generates it. In fact, scripture may even use the past tense for that event because it has happened already in Heaven's reality and timing, at the very least in the mind of God, even though not yet appearing on Earth.

> **Stage 2:** – ***it happens on Earth*** when we experience it in our Time and space.

This two-fold comprehension of Time is fundamental to discerning how our sins can be forgiven in Christ even *before* we commit them on Earth, and how Jesus was himself forgiving sins and healing people in fulfilment of Isaiah 53:4 *before* the actual crucifixion.

2 Timothy 1:9-10 alludes to this Two-Stage Process:

> This grace *was given* us in Christ Jesus *before* the beginning of Time, but it has *now* been revealed through the appearing of our Saviour Christ Jesus, who *has destroyed death* (right away, but applied fully in our future) and has brought life and *immortality* to light through the gospel.

We see that grace to cover our sins was provided in Heaven's Time before the making of our planet, before Time in our Universe had even begun! And that death has also been destroyed, such that we are right now immortal when accepting the gospel of salvation through Jesus!

How incredibly secure that makes us in Christ—having already been granted eternal life regardless of what happens to us in our world.

God's grace was subsequently revealed *on Earth* only when Jesus came.

This was the same provision (grace) but at two different periods in two different Venues – first in Heaven, then much later on Earth.

You and I are both affected by God's dual start of many processes.

Even simple questions like "when does life begin?" necessitate both stages for a full answer.

Stage 1: – our life begins when God decides and designs it in Heaven.
Stage 2: – our life begins when we are formed in the womb on Earth.

We see both of these stages extraordinarily clearly in Jeremiah 1:5, "*Before* I formed you in the womb, I knew you—*before* you were born, I set you apart." God knew Jeremiah before the prophet was born on our planet!! You cannot know someone who does not exist already—Jeremiah was in existence, in a way we do not yet comprehend.

Our own double beginning is seen clearly in Psalm 139: 15-16, where as you may recall my own thinking along these lines first began:

> When I was woven together in the depths of the Earth,
> your eyes saw my unformed body;
> all the days ordained for me *were written* in your book
> *before* one of them came to be.

Verse 16 becomes more impacting if I put in the Venues:

> All the days ordained for me (to live on Earth)
> were written in your book (in Heaven)
> before one of them came to be (on Earth).

We do not understand in what way we pre-existed such that God knew us before we were conceived physically on Earth. But we do know from scripture that God knew Jeremiah, Esau, Jacob, Isaac, Josiah and others before they were born in our world.

Many exciting revelations await us in the afterlife!

Let's apply Two-Stage understanding to the important biblical account of Abraham and Sarah, which is accepted by Jews, Christians and Muslims.

God told Abraham and Sarah that they were to have a son in a year "and you will call him Isaac... whom Sarah will bear to you by this time next year" (Genesis 17:19,21). In this case Isaac was not yet conceived on Earth and it would be a full year before he was born. But Isaac existed in Heaven already, certainly in the innovative planning of God, and his name (meaning laughter) had even been chosen for him by God, just as God "knew" Jeremiah before his birth. Perhaps Isaac's name was chosen by Father God to reflect the joy of this elderly couple having their own son at last; or to remind Sarah that she had laughed at the unlikely prospect of bearing a child at an advanced age?

What is more, we see that through Isaac, God promised to make Abraham a "father of many nations" and said: "I will make nations of you, and kings will come from you" (Genesis 17:6). This is astonishing, because it was hundreds of years before these "kings" appeared in Abraham's line.

So here we have another example of God "calling forth the generations (of people to come) from the *beginning*" (Isaiah 41:4). Abraham's descendants down the centuries would be people not yet in existence on our planet, but who had already been planned and perhaps even named in Heaven by God.

It would seem that a specific plan of God in Heaven constitutes a definitive, creative act of God, regardless of when it is formulated—or when we learn of it—or experience it on Earth.

For some reason, as in the case of Isaac, God's creativity includes the occasional selection of a person's name.

Names carry significance with God. We see this in God's interaction with the barren Sarah and elderly Abraham, aged 99 years. In Genesis 17:5,15-16, God changes the name of Abram to Abraham and Sarai to Sarah. So, Abram (Noble Father) becomes Abraham (Father of Many), and Sarai (Princess) becomes Sarah (Mother of Nations). These name changes were given long before either of their names were appropriate descriptors in our world, when Sarah was still childless in fact.

It is interesting that NDErs can similarly be told the names of their as yet unborn children. For example, Jeanne MK[18] reports an interaction she had with her heavenly helpers during her NDE:

> Then they told me that I needed to go back to take care of my son Adam. I told them I didn't have a son named Adam.
>
> They told me that soon I would.
>
> Three years later, even though I was on the strongest birth control pills available, I had a son; I named him Adam.

In Western culture, the emphasis God places on names may seem strange, but this is more readily understood in certain other cultures. In parts of Africa, babies are only named after extensive observation of the child, in order to determine a name of best fit. In some places cultural identity is perpetuated by children being required to learn and recite the list of names of their own ancestors. I have an Australian friend, who during prayer was told the name she was to give to her son—Joshua, who was yet to be born. Today Joshua is a fine young man.

I had a comparable experience when my pregnant wife Brenda was told on examination by a Doctor in Malawi, but without the benefit of an ultrasound, that our fourth child would likely be a small girl, based on the baby's size and heart rate. My eldest son, who had two sisters already, longed for a brother and burst into tears when we told him that it seemed he would not be getting one.

Later, on my knees in prayer for the upcoming baby, God spoke clearly to me (a rare occurrence) and said, "It will be a boy and you are to name him Jason."

I immediately told Brenda this good news! At once we wondered, why the name Jason? It was not a name we would have chosen, but for some reason still unknown to us, that was what God said he should be named.

I have wondered over the years at the choice of the name Jason. My wife believes the significance of Jason's miraculous healing from meningitis as a newborn is reflected in the meaning of the name, which is "healer" or "healing". She could be right (she generally is), but I'm not sure. Was Jason the name he carried in Heaven before he was born on Earth? Whatever the reason, Jason has proven to be a wonderful son and a joy to us, as have each of our other three children.

Psalm 139 suggests that God has decided the maximum length of time you and I will spend on Earth. We can shorten this by a free-will choice, as in suicide, and thereby spoil God's best plans for us, but we cannot prolong our lives beyond what God has decreed. This is confirmed in Job 14:5,

> A person's days are determined;
> you have decreed the number of his months,
> and have set limits he cannot exceed.

The bottom line is that none of these scriptures make any spiritual sense unless we recognise that all of God's creative acts, from the Universe to individuals to the grace and salvation provided by Jesus, occur first in Heaven, and then only later, sometimes much later, in our Cosmos.

Does an analysis of the Creation account in Genesis provide supporting information for the take-home principle of Two-Stage Theory?

It absolutely does!

> **Stage 1:** – the world was created in Heaven when God decided it; its existence began then, during six days of inventive brilliance. This was its first beginning.
>
> God then rested on the seventh day of Creation in Heaven, and shadowed down this requirement for a day of rest on Earth for our own benefit, because we are created to be like him.
>
> **Stage 2:** – the world was subsequently created in our Universe over a different Time span; its development in our Time and space began to unfurl after this second beginning.
>
> The "Unfolding of Creation", as we may perhaps label God's implementation, was then—and only then—launched!

It is fair to hold the view that Creation, our own selves, and also the grace and salvation provided by Jesus, all had a minimum of two beginnings: one in Heaven, then another subsequently in our Universe, because that is how God does things—as revealed so clearly in the Bible, but not generally understood until this book. And now that we know Time in Heaven is different, a startling revelation about the Venues and the timing of the Creation invades our understanding.

As we look at the Bible through this new prism of Two-Stage Theory, we find fresh understanding about ourselves and our place in the Universe starting to tumble out of its pages.

PART 4

OUR TIME BEGINS

CHAPTER 9

THE WORDS OF CREATION

"Through him all things were made", John 1:3 NIV
—Apostle John introducing the Word (Jesus).

Although I was personally convinced from Psalm 139 that God had created first in Heaven, and then had implemented that Creation later in our Time and space as an ongoing process, I nevertheless wanted to know more from scripture as to when, where, how and especially why he had done so! My search continued and still does.

As I probed the scriptures from Genesis onwards, I made the exciting discovery that three different words had been used in the Hebrew language that had been translated as "create" or "created" in our modern Bibles!

I wondered, would God the Holy Spirit have inspired three different words to be chosen if they were all supposed to carry the same identical meaning?

I had already done word studies in the Bible and acquired enriched understanding by studying the original words and their contexts in scripture. Like many readers, I had studied the different words used in the biblical Greek of the New Testament which have been translated into English as "love", but each carrying their own specific and different meanings. My concept of "love" itself had been greatly enhanced by studying which word had been used in the original. Might the three words of Creation also unlock fresh insight into God's ingenuity?

I slowly and prayerfully checked the use of each of the words as they had been used in the Old Testament. As I had hoped, my comprehension of the Creation process itself grew apace. God's inspired use of Biblical words is intentional and precise in the original text—but, unfortunately, this differentiation does not appear in any English translations.

So as not to fly under false colours, I must emphasise that I am a scholar of neither Hebrew nor Greek. However, Peter Haycock[19] is an expert in Biblical Hebrew and kindly verified my discussion that follows of the three different Hebrew words, translated commonly in our English Bibles as "create", but which can have differing meanings. I have also had the text checked out by different Pastors and Bible Teachers—and while all have been surprised by its content, none has discounted it so far. In fact, a number have embraced the comprehension you will find in these pages. The endorsements at the beginning of this book indicate this.

> To uncover the deeper significance of the Creation, we must investigate the three different words in Hebrew that are often translated as "create" in our modern English Bibles.

Don't panic and think, "I can't possibly grasp Hebrew. I might as well give up now."

Please DON'T.

No understanding in the slightest of Hebrew is needed to uncover the use of the three words in scripture. There are only three of them and no further Hebrew is considered. Our examination of them is entirely in English.

The three words in Hebrew are "bara", "yatzar" and "asah". I will use these three spellings although the same words in different books and contexts can be spelt differently; for simplicity, I am ignoring variants.

Each of the three Creation words has a different emphasis, although they overlap in meaning. It's the overlap that can be translated "to create".

Any of the three may be used if the broad sense of "create" is the only meaning that is intended. However, each carries its own nuances, just as flowers carry different fragrances but are nevertheless all flowers. The word used for "create" in a given sentence may reflect these shades of meaning.

A model will help to clarify their interrelationship.

Suppose a potter wishes to indent a piece of clay as part of moulding it. He pushes down with his finger, but finds the clay too stiff. He calls two friends who overlap their fingers with his and all three push down. The "creative pressure" is applied only where the three overlap, so each is being creative. However, each finger is furthermore bringing its own strengths and weaknesses to the process—they are not the same. The three words for "create" are a bit like the three fingers, as shown in the diagram that follows:

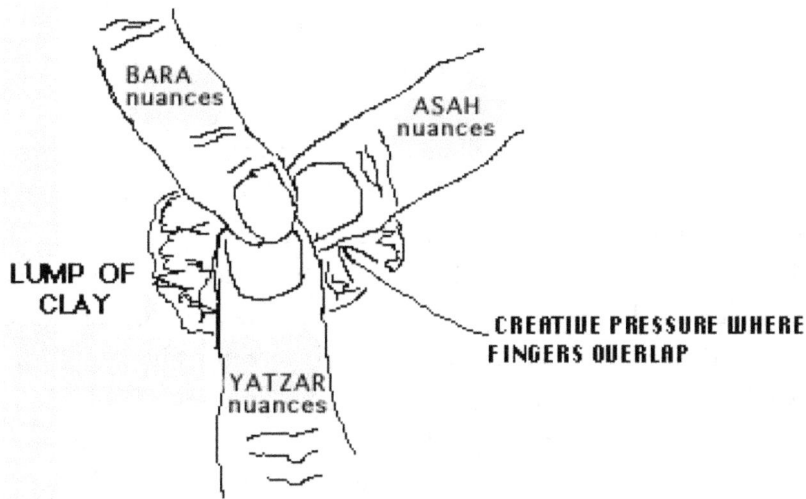

BARA

"Bara" is the first word translated "create" that we meet in the scriptures, in the Bible's opening statement in fact. I will indicate the English word's derivation in brackets. "In the beginning, God created (bara) the heavens and the Earth". (In this case, and in subsequent examples, I will ignore any grammatical variations of the basic Hebrew words and write "bara", "yatzar" or "asah" in the appropriate positions).

"Bara" is a fascinating word because it is reserved to describe God's activity exclusively. Throughout scripture, we find that humankind can "yatzar" and "asah" but never "bara". Perhaps for this reason, many scholars believe it denotes "create out of nothing" as only God can do. While this may be a simplified version of its usage in some passages, in others it describes the Creation of Jerusalem (Isaiah 65:18), of Israel (Isaiah 43:15) and of individual people (Malachi 2:10), all of which, on our planet anyway, involved pre-existent material.

"Bara" is translated at times as "formulated" or "prepared" rather than simply "created", and I feel its deeper meaning is seen in these alternative words. They represent the formative or *design* stages of creating something.

> *"Bara" emphasises the preparation and formulation stages of a creative act of God. It is thereby the initial design stage that launches the act itself.*

Only God's incredible intellect could formulate or design something like the heavens and the Earth, or the other activities we see associated with "bara". It is this that makes "bara" unique and divine.

This association of "bara" with the formative design aspects of God's inventive activity does not mean it is fully replaceable with the word "design".

"Bara" does mean "to create", but is simplified by thinking of it as his "design input" into the creative process. I know of no single English word to convey this meaning adequately. Though it is an oversimplification, many passages are clarified tolerably by translating "bara" as "design" and I will do so on occasion, but please remember that it means more than that. The "preparation" and "formulation" of something new incorporates more than design alone, but it would be clumsy to replace "bara" with two words each time—so "design" will do.

To make a new toy, or cooking implement, mobile phone app, or anything novel, perceptive design is needed as the first practical step. Therefore "bara" is commonly used in scripture to describe the *beginning* of God's resourceful processes, initiating something **new**. For example:

Jeremiah 31:22, describing a fundamental change about to take place, "The Lord will create (bara) a *new* thing on Earth".

Numbers 16:30, "But if the Lord brings about (bara) something totally *new,* and the Earth opens its mouth and swallows them..."

Isaiah 48:6,7, "I will tell you of *new* things, of hidden things unknown to you. They are created (bara) now and not long ago".

Isaiah 65:17, "I will create (bara) *New* Heavens and a *New* Earth".

Please note that God's ingenious design input did not stop in Genesis—it is ongoing and continues until today, and will do so during all our tomorrows.

God is creative—from our experience and biblical knowledge, he always has been, and from prophetic statements that extend into our future, he always will be.

God's active initiation of *new* things is a feature of who he is.

We see this in scripture, for example in Isaiah 48:7 "They are created (bara) *now* and not long ago" and in Psalm 104:24,29,30:

> The Earth is full of your creatures... When you take away their breath, they die and return to the dust. When you send your Spirit, they are created (bara—long tense—continuing process) and you *renew* the face of the ground.

God's Spirit is therefore intimately involved in the cycles of life, death, and new developments that we find currently in our world. The fact that "bara" has been used in the long, continuing tense in the quote above suggests a progression of "redesign" may even be involved—perhaps corresponding to the "adaptation" of Biologists.

I have heard the hollow argument that God stopped working on Day 6 of Creation and has not continued creating, a sort of Christian version of the old secular "God is Dead" philosophy. There are many scriptures to refute this. Consider, as another, Christ's words in John 5:17—"My Father is *always* at his work, to this very day...". NDEs illustrate comprehensively this continuing involvement, and so does answered prayer, fulfilment of prophecies, and the inspired modern miracles that I and many others have had the privilege to investigate or experience for ourselves. Both Brenda and I have had the wonder of miracles happening instantly in our own bodies.

"Bara" does not necessarily mean "created out of nothing" or "Ex Nihilo", but can do so on occasion. Peter Haycock notes that it can mean "made out of nothing previously created"—and the distinction is important. To quote Peter:

> Most Jewish sources suggest that God compressed matter out of his divine energy; that is, vortexed energy into atomic matter rather than that matter cost nothing of God save his spoken thought and design. "Ex Nihilo" has the idea of "out of nothing" but is inadequate compared to the Hebrew word suggesting actual inherent energy, though not derived from the *essence* of God Himself as in the pantheism of Hindu understanding.

Those interested in Astronomy will have noticed the match of the Jewish interpretation with some modern thinking; that atomic material might have condensed out of energy soon after the "Big Bang". While there are difficulties with this simple hypothesis, many still hold to it and in my opinion it is likely to be at least partially correct, but only if it was driven by divine "bara".

YATZAR

"Yatzar" is another Hebrew word commonly translated as "create". It is perhaps easier to understand than "bara". Its noun equivalent is a "potter", and we can picture him working away at his wheel to produce pottery. He takes pre-existent material, such as clay, and "fashions" or "models" it with his hands into the shape he wants. We see this concept very clearly in Isaiah 64:8, "Yet you, LORD, ARE OUR FATHER. We are the clay, you are the potter; we are all the work of your hand". The word used here for the divine "potter" comes from "yatzar".

"Fashioning" and "modelling" are English equivalents for "yatzar".

And "yatzar" can happen in Heaven as well as on our planet. This is essentially the intuitive comprehension I received all those years ago on reading Psalm 139:16 in the King James Bible: "Thine eyes did see my substance yet being imperfect (on Earth)—and in Thy book, all my members (parts) were written (in Heaven), which in continuance were fashioned (yatzar) when as yet there were *none* of them (on Earth)".

This implies that you and I were "yatzar" in Heaven before we were "yatzar" on our world. Perhaps sculptors like Rodin are following God's innovative path without knowing it when preparing clay models first before generating the finished product in bronze or steel.

Other references communicate the concept of God making structures out of pre-existent materials on the Earth itself e.g. when he created man in Genesis 2:7, "The Lord God fashioned (yatzar) the man from the dust of the ground and breathed into his nostrils the breath of life".

This process, to "yatzar" a man, takes time. God does not indicate how long the procedure took him.

We find that God fashions a variety of other material things in a similar way e.g. all kinds of animals (Genesis 2:19), dry land (Psalm 95:5), his people (Isaiah 43:1,7), the Earth (Isaiah 45:18) and mountains (Amos 4:13). In terms of Shadow Theory, certain of these cases may refer to prototypes "fashioned and modelled" in Heaven and brought into existence subsequently in our Universe.

"Yatzar" goes beyond the modelling of material things. We are told about God in Jeremiah 51:19 that he is "the fashioner (yatzar) of all things".

Consequently, we find that God fashions (models) summer and winter (Psalm 74:17), the nation of Israel (Isaiah 43:1), light and darkness (Isaiah 45:7), the spirit of man (Zechariah 12:1), and even a disaster for the disobedient people living in Jerusalem (Jeremiah 18:11).

Humankind, created as a copy of God, can likewise fashion things such as pottery and metal implements. A graphic example is given in Isaiah 44:12, "The blacksmith takes a tool and works with it in the coals; he shapes (yatzar) an idol with hammers".

Unlike "bara", which emphasises God's design element in the creative process, "yatzar" emphasises fashioning and modelling within that process. When God's ingenuity is involved, the two naturally overlap and interrelate in practice, so it is easy to see how they can both be translated as "create".

Functioning together, "bara" and "yatzar" are like two of the overlapping fingers generating creative pressure on the piece of modelling clay in my earlier diagram.

I watched a 3D printer in operation. It followed the computer drawings and dimensions that my engineering friend Geoff had created for it to print out. It did so in shiny plastic. Using these skills, he made us a unique bottle top, his printer taking some hours to follow and complete the precise diagram that he had fed into it. Perhaps this modelling and fashioning process taken together could be likened to "bara" and "yatzar" functioning together. My friend first carried the "bara" in his head, formulating and preparing it, then produced the modelling drawings used to "yatzar" the component that was being printed out. It is now in regular use in our home—thanks Geoff!

But there is more to production than "bara" and "yatzar". The printer that was working the black glossy plastic to enact Geoff's design was vital. Without its *actions*, that component would not have been created as a tangible, practical object, but would have remained in the design and modelling stages.

Take another simple example, say the production of a new type of car: "yatzar" can be likened to the computer modelling of components necessary for the overall design "bara". But what about the many steps required to actually assemble the car, whereby the design (bara) and modelling (yatzar) will result in the completed car itself?

The first two aspects of the creative process, "bara" and "yatzar", are embodied within the third important and distinctive word of Creation—"asah".

"Asah" is the third finger supplying creative pressure.

ASAH

This third Hebrew word "Asah" is found translated into English as "create" in the Old Testament. It is a far more general word than the other two. In its simplest sense, it means "actioned". Translators may look at surrounding words and choose what they suppose the particular "action" was and use the appropriate English word. For example, suppose a text read "The man 'asah' with his sword", one translator might select "struck" and another "poked" while another "slashed" and a fourth "swung". Making a choice of an appropriate word is necessary because English is far richer in action words than Hebrew, but it does introduce a great degree of uncertainty about the intended meaning of the original text.

Because "asah" is such a wide-ranging word, it is far more common in scripture than either "bara" or "yatzar". Where it is used to describe an aspect of the Creation, the general verbs "made" and "did", or the noun "work" are further common translations. For example, Isaiah 64:8 reads:

> Yet you, LORD, are our Father.
> We are the clay, you are the potter (yatzar);
> we are all the work (asah) of your hand.

Note that "asah" in this case is describing a very wide-ranging overall action, the Creation of each individual person. But "asah" can additionally be used to describe the thousands of separate actions that God performs over a period of Time—as components of that overall action—kind of an action sequence or "action plan".

Continuing with the Creation of a man to illustrate this: Genesis 1:26 states, "Let us make (asah) man in our image". Therefore, God had an overall action plan to be achieved, the Creation of humankind as an expression of himself! But this comprised many individual actions, a few of which are seen in Proverbs 20:12, Ecclesiastes 7:29, Job 31:15, Job 10:9.

These verses illustrate that God is involved in planning parenthood, creating within the womb long before the birth of a baby.

Thereby we see that to "asah" a complicated system, such as making you, there was a general aspect, the overall target action plan to be achieved, and many specific individual actions that taken together generated you.

In terms of Two-Stage Theory, developments and adaptations on Earth may implement the "bara", "yatzar" and "asah" stages that began in Heaven in heavenly Time.

There are a number of important descriptions in the Bible that illustrate both the *general* and the *specific* nature of the word "asah".

Consider the Lord's instructions concerning the building of a tabernacle (tent) in which God planned to live among the Israelites wandering in the desert. He begins with the general aspect, the overarching target to be achieved, when he commands, "Make (asah) this tabernacle and all its furnishings exactly like the pattern (plan) I will show you"—sort of an overall operational "action plan" (Exodus 25:9). He then proceeds to give dozens of strikingly specific instructions how to make (asah) the individual components of that tabernacle. e.g. "Have them make (asah) an ark of acacia wood—two and a half cubits long, a cubit and a half wide, and a cubit and a half high. Overlay it with pure gold, both inside and out, and make a gold moulding around it. Cast four gold rings for it and fasten them to its four feet, with two rings on one side and two rings on the other"... etc. etc.

Why are God's instructions so meticulous? Hebrews 8:1-2 explains:

> Now the main point of what we are saying is this: We do have such a high priest (Jesus), who sat down at the right hand of the throne of the Majesty in Heaven, and who serves (still today) in the sanctuary, *the true tabernacle set up by the Lord, not by a mere human being.*

The earthly tent was to be a copy, as per Shadow Theory, of the sacred one already standing in Heaven, of "the true tabernacle set up by the Lord, not by a mere human being."

Why did God want the copy on Earth to imitate so precisely the tent in Heaven? Perhaps the answer is that God intended to visit this tent and even live in it as the Israelites wandered in the desert, sort of a sacred home from home:

> "The people must make a sacred Tent for me, so that I may live among them" (Exodus 25:8 in Good News Bible).

The "asah" therefore was described in great detail to ensure a true copy of God's heavenly tent.

On a deeper level, it was "sacred" and each component and dimension carried significance, and an inaccurate copy would have incorrectly prefigured Christ's coming into our world and living amongst us. This prefiguring has been written about by commentators but is beyond the focus of this book. Suffice to say, God's plans, prepared in Heaven to be actioned or "asah" later in our world, were meticulous and seemed to carry significance beyond the actual physical construction.

Despite the input of the best of skilled and inspired workers, the tabernacle still took seven months to build (create) using the heavenly instructions.

Once it was completed, God's presence as a cloud and a pillar of fire came to the tabernacle and he lived there amongst the Israelites for a while during their wanderings.

The tabernacle was not "bara" just prior to being built on our planet, nor was the temple "bara" later on, because they both pre-existed in Heaven already and presumably had been "bara" there long before God sent instructions how man should copy and "asah" them on Earth.

INTERPLAY OF THE CREATION WORDS IN SCRIPTURE

To see if my comprehension of the Creation words was valid, I checked it against every occurrence of "bara" and "yatzar" in scripture. My understanding held up. I also checked out nearby usages of "asah", without uncovering problems. However, I did not check out every usage of "asah" that was not associated with "bara" or "yatzar", because there were too many.

To illustrate their interplay, I will describe a couple of examples.

Isaiah 43:6,7 uses the Creation words in sequence—of design preceding modelling and actions.

> Bring my sons from afar
> and my daughters from the ends of the Earth—
> everyone who is called by my name,
> whom I created (bara) for my glory,
> whom I formed (yatzar) and made (asah)."

We find the above succession in other places too—from designing to modelling to production—in particular during the six days of Creation in Genesis and beyond.

In Genesis 6:5-7—God's actions and design sequencing are intertwined:

> The LORD saw how great the wickedness of the human race had become on the Earth, and that every inclination of the thoughts of the human heart was only evil all the time. The LORD regretted that he had made (asah—overall completed action) human beings on the Earth, and his heart was deeply troubled. So, the LORD said, "I will wipe from the face of the Earth the human race I have created (bara)—and with them the animals, the birds and the creatures that move along the ground—for I regret that I have made (asah) them."

God is certainly a stickler for detail where things are important to him. I can picture a great artist and scientist such as God building the Cosmos and

Earth progressively, based on a heavenly action plan, equivalent to how the tabernacle was "asah".

This same process of an overall action plan proceeding from Heaven, is seen elsewhere in scripture too:

> *In the building of Noah's ark.* God gives Noah an overall "asah" action plan to be achieved, to "make (asah) yourself an ark of cypress wood." (Genesis 6:14). He then follows with a series of very specific progressive "asah" instructions similar to those for the tabernacle. In Genesis 6:22 we look back at the result with another general statement—"Noah did (asah) everything just as God commanded him". Precise accuracy was especially important because the ark prefigured God's plan of salvation for humankind (1Peter 3:19-22).

> *In the building of the temple.* We read the specific actions (asah) that Solomon did to make the temple in 1Kings 6 & 7, and this is concluded by looking back at the general accomplishment with these words in 1Kings 7:51—"When all the work King Solomon had done (asah) for the temple of the Lord was finished, he..." This temple was a copy of that in Heaven in which Christ ministers to this day (Hebrews 9:23-25).

We find further aspects of God's inventive sequences described in Jeremiah 10:12, "God made the Earth by his *power*, he founded the world by his *wisdom* and stretched out the heavens by his *understanding*".

In other words, there is hugely more to God's ingenious creative processes in scripture than we find in the action words "bara", "yatzar" and "asah", but we are limiting ourselves in this book to the interplay between these three key Creation words.

In all of this, we perceive that God is not haphazard. His innovative actions have continued to be planned thoroughly and in great detail in advance, just as when he in Heaven created the Universe.

Having determined their meaning and colossal importance, I next zeroed in to investigate the usage of these three different words for "create" in the highly contentious first two chapters of Genesis. I found that they helped immensely to explain the fundamental sequences of the account of the Creation.

The discoveries that I made were new to Creation literature and delighted me. I hope you also find them inspiring.

CHAPTER 10

GENESIS UNLOCKED: KEY WORDS OF CREATION

"In the beginning God..."

—Genesis 1:1 NIV

Genesis and our true origins become much more accessible when looked at in terms of the different nuances that the three Hebrew words for "create" bring to it.

We must at the same time take note of the Hebrew and Greek (Septuagint) tenses, which were applied to all three of the words translated as "create". The long continuing tense was often employed in Hebrew to denote an aspect of an action that had not yet been completed, but had begun and was continuing into the future. Unfortunately, the first Bible translators into modern languages, believing that the whole of Creation was already a completed "done deal" in our Universe, repeatedly ignored this use of the continuing Hebrew tense in the text, and translated the events in the simple past tense instead, denoting completion. For example, when our Genesis text in English reads: "God created the stars" it would be already a completed event during the six days of Creation—but since in the Hebrew the long continuing "future" tense was used, I believe it more closely denotes an action plan started in Heaven that was to continue. To this day, astronomers watch new stars being formed.

The actual text reads: He also made ("asah"—long tense—an action plan made first in Heaven that continues even now) the stars (Genesis 1:16).

Because innovative design initiates something new, "bara" is generally used to describe the start of God's creative processes; for example, Genesis starts with this overarching statement:

> In the beginning, God "bara" the heavens and the Earth.

The rest of Chapter 1 of Genesis describes his "bara" in daily detail in Heaven, where he was operating from, and where he rested on the seventh heavenly day. It is followed by the action plans (asah) whereby he intended to implement his designs.

Here is another example taken from Genesis 1:27, which describes the initial act in the Creation of humankind.

> In the image of God he created ("bara") them;
> male and female he created ("bara") them.

Later, from Genesis 2:4, he starts to expand on how he put this "bara" into practice when subsequently forming and guiding humankind in our world. The "bara" in chapter 1 was "male and female he created ("bara") them", but they were not "yatzar" until when Adam first, then afterwards Eve, were made specifically.

The designs that had been set up in Genesis Chapter 1 were finished before Day 7 in Heaven, but we see only in Chapter 2 how they began to be implemented with respect to mankind on our planet.

Certainly, the Universe and Earth were not yet in existence when God initially "bara" them in Heaven in the first verse of Genesis, and "asah" and "yatzar" were still to unfold.

Because God resides in Heaven, the design (bara) aspect of his creative act begins there. Its implementation or "second beginning" in our Cosmos starts later.

This process illustrates the principle that once God has spoken, his word will not return to him empty or unproductive (Isaiah 55:11). From where do you suppose God was sending his word, the word that *returns* to him?

Notice that the word God sends out "will accomplish" (future tense) what it is that he desires.

The sequential Creation of the Earth itself can be visualised like this:

> ***God "bara" and "asah" the Earth in Heaven***
> ***where it has its first beginning.***

↓

> ***The Earth has its second beginning*** (*with all three Creation words bara, asah and yatzar involved*) ***in our Universe according to God's word—which thereby was not unproductive.***

↓

> ***The Earth continues its advance. This developmental process could include Evolution as well as instantaneous productions—as and if decided by God.***

Although design order is distinctive from order of appearance, the Bible does not necessarily tell us the relationship between the design sequence in Heaven and the order or timings that these intentions were accomplished in our Cosmos.

The wording in Genesis and elsewhere in scripture suggests that from the start, God intended to create humankind on Earth *to resemble himself,* which would comprise his overall operational plan or "asah".

From this, we deduce a vital principle for comprehending God's workings on many different levels on our planet, including Creation and Evolution. As we have established previously:

> *God is purpose-focused and the record in scripture*
> *may range widely and suddenly through Time.*

Bearing God's overall purpose in mind, *with humankind in view*, we find the Creation order of Genesis 1 to be an entirely logical design sequence: first the Universe and the world, then light energy on which all life forms on the Earth would ultimately depend, then land and sea for them to live on or in, then plant life as the basis of food webs, then the sun to provide an ongoing supply of essential light energy for photosynthesis as well as to establish cycles of Time, then animal life—and ultimately when everything was ready and in place—humankind.

Over several years, I ran simple competitions with my senior Science students (all boys) at the end of the academic year once formal work had been completed. All of us, students included, are designed as reflections of God, and I wondered how they would meet the challenge I gave them. I set them to design a habitable planet for new life forms of their own design, but on an imaginary planet that would support these new life forms—planning and scientific thinking required! As fewer than a hundred students ultimately completed the task it was hardly valid as research, nor was it supposed to be, as I did it for my interest alone. I then asked them to label and number their diagrams in the order in which the features had been drawn.

The students' overall results were quite close to the order given in Genesis 1, though not close to what scientists believe has developed on Earth.

Most students firstly drew a planet, some with weird shapes like donuts etc., then water for survival was common, then some form of vegetation or other life forms—but few devised an energy source such as the sun at all, and those who did added it towards the end of their plans.

The order that God later chose to accomplish his intentions in our world varied slightly from his original design sequence, similar to how the order of the chapters in this book differs from my original pencil notes where it was first formulated and planned.

When a couple plan a dream home, few would start by planning the foundations in detail—yet we all know that that is where the actual construction of the home begins.

Similarly, the fossil record suggests a reverse order for the appearance of some forms of life on Earth than we find in the planning description in Genesis 1: birds in Genesis 1:20 were planned before land animals in verse 24, although Palaeontologists suggest the birds may have developed from land-dwelling dinosaurs; and vegetation and fruit trees in Genesis 1:11 came before the sun in Genesis 1:16. Plants, however, need sunshine to thrive and to make their food.

In the verses that follow, the "heavens" (plural) written about denote our Universe, and not God's Heaven.

The phrase "God 'bara' the heavens and the Earth" in Genesis 1 is followed by the actions (asah) that he planned so as to accomplish his design for those heavens. We learn that "God 'asah' the great expanse" in verse 7. "God 'asah' two great lights", denoting our sun and moon, and "He also 'asah' the stars", both in verse 16. These "asah" were the action plans he would employ when later on putting his designs into practice.

And what about timing? Suppose a new shopping complex is planned; there will be a time differential between the architect's design and computer modelling stages, and a further delay before the action plan is put into practice on the ground. God's creative planning unfolded likewise.

As in other scriptures quoted already, 2 Kings 19:25 reveals this sequential process. God is speaking about his dealings with Assyria:

> Long ago I "asah" it, in days of old I "yatzar" it, *now* I have brought it to pass (on Earth).

This wording clearly indicates a time lapse between God's action plan of "long ago", his modelling "in days of old"—and its subsequent dynamic fruition in our world "*now* have I brought it to pass".

We note that is God himself who is teaching us about this Time differential—between his planning in Heaven, and the implementation of his plans in our world.

It follows that, because God does not prescribe the specific timing that his plans would be implemented on Earth, nor the methodology he would employ, Young-Earth Creation and Old-Earth Creation may both remain feasible models for the timing of the Creation in our Cosmos.

Creation of Our Future Universe

I wondered whether I could gain insights into the Creation of our Universe by considering the prophesied Creation of the next one—the New Heavens, with its New Earth and New Jerusalem? I found this to be an exciting concept, with a confidence arising from studying the detailed accuracy of God's previously fulfilled prophecies. God is progressively creative and innovative, in each of our lives also!

It is noteworthy that the Bible opens by describing the Creation of the first Heavens and Earth, and closes by describing his Creation of New Heavens and a New Earth that are still to appear.

I soon discovered that we glean significant principles by studying both.

Isaiah 65:17,18 (written around 700 BC) introduces the New Heavens and New Earth as biblical forecasts spoken by God, but still in the design stage because "bara" is used.

> "See, I will create (bara)
> New Heavens and a New Earth.
> The former things will not be remembered,
> nor will they come to mind.
> But be glad and rejoice forever
> in what I will create (bara),
> for I will create (bara) Jerusalem to be a delight
> and its people a joy."

Unfortunately, this passage, as above in the NIV, is often translated in the future as God "will create" as it refers to the New Heavens, New

Earth and New Jerusalem, based on their anticipated future manifestation to mankind. However, the Hebrew language uses the participle "creating", suggesting the present tense—a process that is underway. This denotes an action that was likely continuing at the time of writing, around 700 BC i.e. the translation of verse 17 should start something like: "I am 'bara' (creating, designing) New Heavens and a New Earth".

The Good News Bible recognises this in its translation: The LORD SAYS, "I *am making* (i.e. not yet a finished product) a New Earth and New Heavens."

Consider again what the Apostle John wrote in Revelation 21:1-2, nearly eight centuries after the above prophecy had been given through Isaiah.

> Then I *saw* a "New Heaven and a New Earth", for the first Heaven and the first Earth had passed away, and there was no longer any sea. I *saw* the Holy City, the New Jerusalem, coming down *out of Heaven* from God, *prepared* as a bride beautifully dressed for her husband.

Even if John was being shown a vision, the New Heaven and New Earth must at the very least have been in an advanced stage of design—suggested further by their detailed descriptions in Revelation 21:10 – 22:6.

God chose Heaven as his location for designing the New Heavens, the New Earth and the New Jerusalem which would one day come down *"out of Heaven"*. This should be no surprise because Heaven is where he lives and Heaven is where he designed our original Universe and Earth. There has been no departure from the way he creates things. He has been entirely consistent. It has been the translators who have been inconsistent and not the Bible.

The New Heavens and the New Earth may even now be physical realities waiting to be manifested, or they may remain "mental models" in the design phase –we do not know exactly in which stage they exist today. Either way, they "exist" from God's perspective, in Heaven nowadays, and they will appear to humankind in our future—because our God has said so—and that he will change his home to the New Jerusalem that will come down out of Heaven onto the New Earth (Revelation 21:1-3).

A significant number of NDErs, for example New Zealand Pastor Ian McCormack[20], believe they too have been shown during their NDE the

New Earth as a beautiful planet-in-waiting, but whether what they were shown was a vision or the completed physical New Earth is not yet clear. Nevertheless, as Ian wrote to me in 2015:

> "*Many* NDErs have seen this New Earth which they share about with me. Over the past 33 years I have met thousands of people who have seen what I saw. I don't believe as some teach that this old Earth will be remodelled into the new one."

Ian is a New Zealander known as "The Box Jellyfish Man" because he died after extensive stings from that most lethal of poisonous sea animals. He was an atheist before being stung and had no biblical knowledge about the New Heavens and the New Earth. He is not a sensationalist. He has been profoundly affected by his experiences and his whole life has been turned around as a result. He describes the New Earth as staggeringly beautiful. Like Ian and countless others, and hopefully you also, I look forward to being there.

It is exciting that the other NDErs, who claim that God showed them the New Earth and New Jerusalem during their experiences in the afterlife, without exception, describe them as visually spectacular.

Consider the biblical description of the New Jerusalem, which is created to be our future city after Judgement (Revelation 21:2):

> I saw the holy city, the New Jerusalem, coming down *out of Heaven*, from God, prepared as a bride *beautifully dressed* for her husband.

The descriptions of the New Jerusalem, which start in verse 10 of Chapter 21, are detailed, far more so than the happenings on any of the days of Creation in Genesis. The city is huge, a stunning cubic structure over 2000 kilometres in length, breadth and height. It will be breathtaking.

The significant number of NDErs who have described the New Jerusalem is noteworthy. They use words very similar to those found in Revelation 21:10 – 22:6 to describe its grandeur. Some of them, especially atheists and other non-Christians, state that they had not read those descriptions in Revelation before seeing the city for themselves and describing its structure, including the gates and walls with lines of precious glowing stones, and its overall shining majesty.

THE PURPOSE THAT DRIVES CREATION

The original Creation and the new one to come are impossible to appreciate unless we grasp this one pivotal fact:

> *Creation had a purpose that predated the planning of Genesis 1.*
> *This purpose "drove" the process.*

In Isaiah 45:18, we glimpse this overarching objective woven in with the unfolding of Creation:

> For this is what the LORD says—
> he who created (bara) the heavens,
> he is God;
> he who fashioned (yatzar) and made (asah) the Earth,
> he founded it;
> he did not create (bara) it to be empty,
> but formed (yatzar) it **to be inhabited**

Right from the design stage God's **purpose** was to make a planet that would not be "empty", but on which life would exist!

When Genesis 1:1 starts, "In the beginning, God 'bara' the heavens and the Earth", it incorporates his objective that it was being designed to be inhabited.

CREATION WORDS AND HUMANKIND

The Creation of humankind was always God's intention for our world.

By verse 16 of Genesis 1, God had finished planning the inanimate Universe and the Earth as far as plant life. He was then ready to begin creating animal life, intending it to be radically different and to culminate in humankind reflecting himself.

He started by planning animal life for the oceans and birds for the land. Verse 21 tells us, "So God created (bara) the great creatures of the sea and every living thing with which water teems and that moves about in it, according to their kinds, and every winged bird according to its kind". This was during Day 5 in Heaven.

When we reach verse 24 and Day 6 in Heaven, we find God listing further land creatures he planned to produce, "each according to their kinds". This is followed with a statement of completion in Heaven, or perhaps of looking back—"And it was so." In verse 25 God made (asah) the wild animals according to their kinds, the livestock according to their kinds, and all the creatures that move along the ground according to their kinds. And God saw that it was all good.

God was then ready to launch on the pinnacle of his Creation—mankind.

He announces his overall action to be achieved in verse 26, "Let Us make (asah – long tense in Hebrew, which suggests an ongoing action into the future) humankind in Our image, in Our likeness, so that they may rule over the fish in the sea and the birds in the sky, over the livestock and all the wild animals, and over all the creatures that move along the ground".

The plural "Our image" is employed because each member of the Trinity was present—Father God, Jesus, and the Holy Spirit.

Having proclaimed this overall intention, his grand "action plan", God embarked on the design stage in Heaven. Verse 27 reads:

> So God created (bara) humankind in his own image,
> in the image of God he created (bara) them;
> male and female he created (bara) them.

From here on we find the words "asah" and "yatzar" are used when describing the processes whereby God achieves these designs, when creating humankind on Earth. For example, Genesis 2:7 reads, "the Lord God formed (yatzar) the man from the dust of the ground and breathed into his nostrils the breath of life, and the man became a living being". Further on in verses 18 and 19 we read, "I will create (asah) an helper for him", which led ultimately to the forming of Eve.

And so, friends, all humankind shares these same two beginnings, the first the "bara" of God in Heaven, the second achieved only later, in his "yatzar" and "asah" of humankind on our world.

Now that we know our true origin, our beginnings, first in Heaven and now later on Earth, we can cautiously begin to approach answers to the question: Why? Why did God make me?

Objections to looking so carefully at the original words and tenses in the Bible is that we are making it "too complicated" and "we should just take Genesis at face value since whichever you look at it, God created."

However, it is translators who have rendered Genesis in our modern versions a whole lot simpler than the original text. What are we wanting: unintentional error or accurate rendering? Do we want to leave forever unresolved, and for some people faith-destroying, issues such as the Creation/Evolution debate?

The Bible was written for our benefit—not for God's benefit, but for ours—and so putting in the hard yards to comprehend it is prudent and life-sustaining.

To summarise my approach to understanding our true origin and God's production processes:

> *By reading with fuller comprehension the words describing God's creating, we perceive his production processes more accurately, and especially can differentiate the design and action **planning** stages (in Heaven) and the **implementation** of these (later, on our Earth).*

For the remainder of this book, my use of the word Creation should be understood to incorporate God's design (bara), modelling (yatzar) and active implementation (asah) stages.

I will unfold my conviction that from the beginning, God's Creation incorporated a progressive, rather than completed, implementation in our

Cosmos that *continues* until today. This implementation may be inclusive of Evolution. It is certainly inclusive of ourselves.

Regarding the Creation, we have emphasised the Where and How. Let's now look in more detail at the Days of Creation that took place in Heaven with particular regard to the When and Why—and marvel afresh—because we are all a part of God's Creation.

CHAPTER 11

THE DAYS OF CREATION
(GENESIS 1:1 TO 2:3)

All of our tomorrows are God's yesterdays

—Richard Sigmund[21]

The Bible is a spiritual book, inspired by God, and we need to turn to God's Spirit to be our Teacher to lead us into deeper truths from it. From relationship comes revelation. We learn most by approaching God in a humble, obedient, and prayerful relationship, while a further aspect to learning is to realise that, as part of our development, God wants us to dig out deeper and deeper truths in scripture, even if concepts are hard to grasp.

Don't believe those who claim scripture is straightforward and should be interpreted in the most obvious way, the simplest interpretation. There would not be so many differing doctrinal positions based on the Bible if its interpretation were so straightforward. Why do the thousands of Christian denominations and groups have different ideas about the future taken from the same biblical prophecies, if it were all so simple?

The reality is that Bible truths can be very difficult to interpret, and in places impossible without the help of its true author, the Holy Spirit, to guide and lead us into the truth that we need to live our lives with and for God.

When we presume to depend entirely on logic to apprehend the depths of the Bible, we have already lost our way. Logic is related to our Universe and life on our planet, and has been given us to negotiate living in our Cosmos, but often falls very short when applied to spiritual experiences and truths.

The Creation in Genesis is an account containing spiritual truth which requires more than logic to grasp it at its centre—it is more like an onion; to view its core there are layers to be peeled away first.

We are now approaching its core.

Please keep in mind that the main thrust of the first two chapters of Genesis is not the times or timings involved, but God's intentions for his Creation.

> "Surely as I *have* planned, so it *will* be, and as I *have* purposed, so it *will* happen" (Isaiah 14:24).

Let's insert into this verse the concept of Creation first in Heaven, followed by Creation in our Cosmos:

> "Surely as I have planned (Creation in Heaven), so it will be (Creation of the Universe), and as I have purposed (Creation in Heaven), so it will happen (Creation on Earth)."

From God's point of view, Creation was completed before it was launched in our Time and space.

That his plans cannot be defeated is emphasised powerfully in Isaiah 14:26,27:

> "This is the *plan* determined for the whole world; this is the hand stretched out over all nations. For the Lord Almighty has *purposed*, and who can thwart him? His hand is stretched out, and who can turn it back?"

Genesis 1:1 – "In the *beginning* God created (bara—short tense, completed action) the heavens and the Earth."

In terms of the timing of the Creation, what does the word "beginning" refer to? We must look to other scriptures for clues.

God's eternal wisdom is one characteristic of who he is, and, of course, was foundational to the beginning in Heaven of his Creation of our Cosmos. In Proverbs 8:23, Amplified Bible, we learn that –

> "[Wisdom] was inaugurated and ordained from everlasting, from the *beginning*, *before* ever the Earth existed."

The first "beginning" of our Universe therefore featured God's wisdom in the planning stages "before ever the Earth existed".

Day 1 of the Creation initiates several important structures:

> Now the Earth was formless and empty, darkness was over the surface of the deep and the Spirit of God was hovering over the waters. And God said, "Let there be light" and there was light. God saw that the light was good, and he separated the light from the darkness. God called the light "day" and the darkness he called "night". And there was evening, and there was morning—the first day (Day 1). Genesis 1:2

"Day 1" is the literal translation, although it is usually translated "the first day". Most likely it refers to Day 1 of God's creative endeavours in Heaven.

Take note please that God himself introduced the concept of a "day" before even mentioning the Sun to control it or humankind to live by it. Logically, it must refer to the first day in Heaven where God was busily formulating his Creation plans rather than a 24-hour Earth day. Read the other numbered "days" in Genesis 1 from the same viewpoint, that these are taking place in Heaven.

Similarly, when we read that God "saw that the light was good", it does not mean that he did not know all about light already! It means that he saw it would be "good" for the world he was designing. Most specifically, it would be good for humankind. It would sustain life and help us to exercise the responsible dominion over the planet that he intended.

This same foreknowledge applies to everything else he was designing to implement on Earth, many features of which were to be Shadows of Heaven, to help prepare us for our distant futures.

There are other New Testament descriptions regarding the Creation that support a concept of pre-design in Heaven. The very word used for the Creation or formation of the world in Revelation 13:8, Ephesians 1:4 and in 1Peter 1:20 is derived from two Greek words that mean taken together, literally, "to throw down"—the design coming *down* from God in his Heaven.

This is supported by Hebrews 11:3 which says, "By faith we understand that the Universe was formed at God's command, so that what is seen was not made out of what was visible".

Each of the first six days of Creation in Heaven is concluded with a statement such as: "And there was evening, and there was morning—the first day."

Although we saw earlier that there are scriptures supporting the concept of "days", "nights", "hours" and "years" in Heaven, we have here the suggestion of mornings and evenings there.

Professor Stoner[22] offers an alternative understanding:

> The (Hebrew) words translated "morning" and "evening" may also mean "beginning" and "ending".
>
> Thus, "And the evening and the morning were the first day" may also mean "And the beginning and ending of this work was the first period (Day) of God's time in creating."

Could presumptions and word choices by translators regarding the Creation have influenced the choice of "morning" and "evening" rather than "beginning" and "ending" for each Day of Creation in Heaven?

However it is read, the "mornings" and "evenings" of the first three days of Creation in Genesis could not have been on Earth, because God set up our earthly days with their dependence on the sun only on Day 4 of his creating. "Mornings" and "evenings" are produced entirely by the sun and the spin of the Earth—hence they could not have been occurring on Earth before the sun was in the sky.

The remaining days of Creation all follow a similar pattern. Each day begins with "And God said…". Thereby, God states an intention for that day's work in Heaven.

God develops the plan from his opening statement to the completion of that day in Heaven's activity, which often expands on his original declaration.

By the end of Day 3, God had designed the inanimate Earth and the vegetation that would develop on it.

Note that during the first day God had decided both light and darkness were to be features of our planet, and to be separated, but to this point he had not revealed the mechanics whereby he would achieve this. Day 4 deals with planning the sun, moon and stars.

> And God said, "Let there be lights in the vault of the sky to separate the day from the night, and let them serve as signs to mark sacred times, ***and days*** and years, and let them be lights in the vault of the sky to give light on the Earth." And it was so. God made (asah—long tense) two great lights—the greater light (sun) to govern the day and the lesser light (moon) to govern the night.

The sun, moon and stars were designed to be our timekeepers to mark out days and years on Earth.

The action plan for creating the days in our world was set up on Day 4 of Creation.

And by then, the basic structure of the Cosmos and our world had been decided by God in Heaven. The sun designed on Day 4 would supply the light energy for Earth to enable vegetation, designed already during Day 3, to make its own food using photosynthesis.

The complexities of animal and human life had not yet been designed. The planning of these occupies the final two days of God's inventive activity in Heaven.

Day 6 was devoted entirely to the designing of humanity in God's likeness and included our intended future role on our world.

One statement that is easy to pass by is that God planned humankind to have "every seed-bearing plant on the face of the *whole* Earth"; consequently, God was already planning for man's life beyond the limited area of the Garden of Eden.

After these six heavenly days of innovative brilliance, God decided to have a day of rest in Heaven. A literal translation of the first three verses of Genesis chapter 2 provides a deep comprehension of what happened next. We read (Genesis 2:1-3):

> Thus, the heavens and the Earth were completed in all their vast array.
>
> By the seventh day God had finished the work he had been doing (asah–completed tense), so on the seventh day he rested from all his work.
>
> Then God blessed the seventh day and made it holy, because on it he rested from all the work that he *had created* (bara—completed tense) *to be made* (asah—passive infinitive).

*** **"Created to be made"**, the literal translation in verse Genesis 2:3 above, is ***not*** the translation given in the main text of almost all modern Bibles. In fact, Bibles to this day usually perpetuate the most unfortunate error in biblical translation history by putting all these events in the past tense.

Two get close to the actual scripture – Young's Literal Translation has "he hath ceased from all his work which God *had prepared for making*" – and the Complete Jewish Bible, which has "God rested from all his work which he had created, *so that it itself could produce*".

As examples of inaccurate translations, the King James reads "in it he had rested from all his work which God created and made" and the NIV reads, "He rested from all the work of creating that he had done". These are very misleading because they put all the events in the past tense. No doubt the translators of the KJV presumed that the totality of Creation took six 24-hour Earth days to be completed—which was the prevailing view in the 15th and 16th centuries when the Bible began to be translated into modern languages from ancient Greek, Latin and Hebrew texts.

The literal and true translation instead indicates that God's creative plans and processes were underway "to be made".

Mistranslation of this key verse Genesis 2:3 has hidden answers vital to the Creation/Evolution debate in Christian circles. It is imperative at this late hour that we return to original wording in the Bible.

Of major significance here is the Septuagint Bible translation mentioned previously. This tells us what a group of renowned Hebrew scholars considered this key verse Genesis 2:3 to mean when they translated it from the original Hebrew into the Greek language at least two centuries before the birth of Jesus Christ. Their rendering was much more faithful to the original Hebrew than modern versions because it did not lose the sense of progressive fulfilment. Sir Lee Brenton's[23] English translation of the Septuagint reads:

> *And God blessed the seventh day and sanctified it, because in it he ceased from all his works,* **which God began to do**.

Those ancient Septuagint scholars were far closer to the original wording and intention than we see in most of our modern English translations.

This is entirely consistent with Two-Stage Theory, and ought to resolve the polarised Time and timing issues that have, until now, separated the sincerest of Creation and Evolution believers.

Genesis 2:3 is a pivotal verse. Since it separates the descriptions of the formative stages of Creation, taking place mainly in Heaven, from the descriptions of what happened subsequently, mainly on Earth, it would be more natural to see an end to Chapter 1 there.

The actual Hebrew text has no chapter divisions and no numbering of verses. These are structures that translators have imposed on scripture in comparatively recent times to enable easier referencing. Chapter divisions were suggested around 1227 AD and the numbering of verses in printed Bibles began only in the mid-1500s. In most cases the chosen chapter endings are fine, but in some cases, they can be inappropriate; and, in this case, downright misleading.

Let's consider briefly how "He had created *to be made*" has been achieved on our planet, and continues to be achieved.

It appears likely that Evolution is one of those processes that God has employed. Why might he have invented, designed and applied Evolution? What is special about it?

It is a brilliant process whereby life forms can adapt and change to their environment quickly without constant monitoring. We should all marvel at Evolution in the manner that Dr David Instone-Brewer[24] does:

> Evolution is nature's in-built ability to produce new designs in response to new needs and opportunities. It is much more powerful and flexible than a fixed blueprint. It is an amazing aspect of God's Creation… We should recognise that Genesis ascribes the whole process to God, including the powerful design feature we call Evolution.

Dr David has additional perspectives on God's continuing work on the planet:

> Creation wasn't the end of God's hands-on work. The Bible tells us that he also intervenes with miracles and revelations; and he constantly communicates personally with his people. However,

the fact that only a few things are regarded as miracles in the Bible implies that most of what happens on Earth is due to the natural processes that God has built into his Creation.

Even robots are being built that can evolve nowadays! Artificial intelligence (AI) and self-replicating robots are seen by some conventional Scientists as a possible threat to humanity.

The most famous Scientist in the modern era, Stephen Hawking, warned before his death in 2018 that robots specially programmed to "evolve" by adopting helpful design features and discarding unhelpful ones might threaten the survival of humankind. This is not science fiction, this is Stephen Hawking[25].

Elon Musk, billionaire founder of TESLA and SPACE X, agrees with Hawking. Musk, who stars in the documentary "Do You Trust This Computer?", states during it that an immortal, robot-like dictator could have the power to rule mankind forever. "If AI has a goal and humanity just happens to be in the way, it will destroy humanity as a matter of course without even thinking about it. No hard feelings," Musk said. "It's just like, if we're building a road, and an anthill happens to be in the way. We don't hate ants, we're just building a road. So, goodbye anthill."

Perhaps, but also perhaps not.

In any case, a Universe without purpose, design and planning should be consigned to the scrap heap where it belongs.

The great Scientist Max Planck[26], a father of modern Quantum Physics, perceived this when he wrote:

"In the whole of the Universe, there is no force that is either intelligent or eternal, and we must therefore assume that behind this force there is a conscious, intelligent Mind or Spirit. This is the very origin of all matter."

An awesome, personal, conscious, artistic and scientific intellect is ever so obviously involved in Creation. God's consciousness must be, and is, the first cause of the Creation!

After six days of brilliantly creative achievement in Heaven, God decided to rest for one day. He "shadowed" the same requirement for humankind, that every seventh day should be a day of rest from working, called the "Sabbath day observance" and described well in Exodus 20:11: "For in six days the Lord 'asah' the heavens and the Earth, the sea and all that is in them, but he rested on the seventh day. Therefore, the Lord blessed the Sabbath day and made it holy".

This "Sabbath rest" is thereby a commemoration or copy of a past event in Heaven. God rested from his innovative activity on the seventh day *in Heaven* and he requires us, designed to shadow him, to do likewise on our Earth. This is to our advantage and not to his. Jesus made this clear when he stated, "The Sabbath was made for man, not man for the Sabbath" (Mark 2:27).

This weekly cycle of seven days is presumed to have a solely religious origin because there are no cosmic cycles from which it might have derived. The length of a day, or of a month, or of a year, can be pinned to astronomical measurements of one type or another—but not so the length of the seven-day week. Most of us never give that a thought.

To the initial disbelief of the scientific community, the modern Science of Chronobiology, established by Professor Franz Halberg[27] in the 1940s, has uncovered weekly cycles prevalent in perhaps every life form—plants, animals, and even single cells. For example, the supposedly ancient mermaid's wine-glass alga (Acetabularia mediterranea) functions stubbornly to a weekly cycle, despite scientific attempts to disrupt this, such as exposing it to light for varying periods.

There is no apparent biological reason or evolutionary explanation for the prevalence of these weekly rhythms, which extend to refinements such as the rise and fall of bodily chemicals.

Weekly cycles (termed circaseptans) operate within us too, easy to comprehend since we have been made in God's likeness, and he took time out to rest after six-days of hard work, subsequently telling us to do the same.

But why should other life forms operate with seven-day cycles?

Perhaps God built a weekly cycle within their lives as a commemoration, or even a living signature of his original activity in Heaven?

If six days of work followed by a day of rest is God's intention for humankind, we might expect life to succeed best if this rhythm were to be followed.

This has been challenged and tested by two atheist-leaning revolutions. During the French Revolution in 1793 the week was "decimalised"[28] into ten days, but this failed abysmally and normal weeks were resumed by Napoleon in 1806. Communist Russia[29] went the way of a shorter week—of a rotating 5-day cycle, then a 6-day cycle, to try to increase production. Both failed, as did their search for the most efficient ratio of working days to days of rest. 6:1 produced the best output and they returned in humiliated frustration to the 7-day week.

> *We are therefore at our most efficient as a society when we closely follow God's example and instruction, because this fits best our natural rhythms of life that he created.*

There are other advantages to society following a 6:1 weekly rhythm, including family cohesion and emotional and spiritual benefits on the level of the individual. Currently, the seven-day trading week and consequent shift-work is robbing relationships, including family relationships, of the success and enjoyment they should be experiencing together. The adage of "families that play together stay together", while simplistic, definitely contributes to the goals of family cohesion. The converse is certainly true, that abandoning God's model in this and other respects is often a contributing factor to the discord and fracturing of families.

Escalating levels of stress, exhaustion, frustration and even depression are further outcomes often linked to abandoning a day of rest for individuals and society. It is as Jesus explained: the Sabbath day of rest (one day in seven) is for humankind's ultimate benefit rather than a religious imposition. His words ring out to us over the centuries: "The Sabbath was made for man, not man for the Sabbath." People of course, have supposed to our cost that we know better.

We must wonder, where is the promised utopia that was proclaimed we would enjoy once we abandoned God's day of rest requirement? Why didn't it eventuate? Why did those extravagant promises made to us evaporate so soon?

Societies redefining marriage, embracing sexualisation and gender dysphoria through "education" programs in schools, and removing parental protection for our children, are further recent decisions that are already producing similar and even more disastrous consequences for children and for a stable family life, worldwide. Twisted branches are already producing their twisted and bitter fruit.

We seem not to learn from past mistakes—that God *really* knows best.

PART 5

YOUR GOD—AND YOU

CHAPTER 12

ORIGINS
(GENESIS 2:4 ONWARDS)

Religion has the right to express its opinion in the service of the people, but God in Creation has set us free

—Pope Francis[30]

Most of us wonder about our ancestry at one time or another in our lives.

NDErs regularly meet a group of their ancestors in the afterlife, so the God who arranges those meetings considers ancestry significant. Even Jesus' ancestry, both on Mary's side and on Joseph's, are listed in scripture in Matthew 1:1-17 (Joseph) and Luke 3:23-38 (Mary). This emphasis on family and ancestry has largely been set aside in the West, but is totally understood in Africa, Asia, and some other cultures. It is however experiencing a resurgence in Western culture, in what has become a splintering society, with people hoping to find meaning and who they *truly* are through ancestry searches and meeting long lost relatives. DNA analysis can become part of this search for meaning, though for most it is a largely impersonal approach.

Much more exciting than our ancestral identity is our God-given one, and our past and future from his perspective.

God's purpose in creating the Earth rings out from Isaiah 45:18—

> For this is what the LORD SAYS—
> he who created the heavens,
> he is God;
> he who fashioned and made the Earth,
> he founded it;
> *he did not create it to be empty,*
> *but formed it to be inhabited.*

Many scientific papers recognise that for our planet to be inhabited successfully by living plants and animals, a substantial number of physical and chemical conditions had to be present and needed to interact in complex ways that remain mysterious. Carbon-based life forms require a delicately balanced set of circumstances. The fossil record suggests that a significant number of species arose, flourished, and subsequently died out or became unimportant in comparison to other life forms. They were interesting, perhaps even experimental, but not the ultimate intention that God had for the Earth.

The ultimate intention for our world, as we already know, was to provide a home for humans made in God's image—for you and me!

The precise timing, nuts and bolts of how God set about achieving his purposes for the Creation are not specified in scripture, nor attempted in this book. Purpose decides process with God—as per usual.

Acknowledging God's eternal purposes in the scriptures, we recognise that humankind was intended to be the pinnacle of God's design for planet Earth. Consequently, modern humans populated our planet only when it was in a suitable condition for our continuous habitation of it.

The account given in Genesis 2:4 onwards of the beginning of humankind has caused debate down the centuries. Jewish sages and a number of Christians have supposed it to be a parable, rather than a literal account. Parables exist in the Old Testament and Jesus taught in parables. Parables are illustrative stories unlikely to be literally true in respect to their details, but are designed to communicate spiritual truths, which are far more important. This may be the case with the account of Adam and Eve; it certainly reads like a parable in places and every adult can identify with its message of temptation, sin, guilt and separation from God.

Nevertheless, the account could be true literally, and it is from this standpoint that I will approach it.

In support of this decision, I noticed that when Adam is mentioned in the New Testament, the references appear to be to a literal person rather than to a representative character of humankind in a parable. For example, Paul mentions Adam (Romans 5:14) and a reference in Jude regards Adam as the first man (Jude 14), as does Luke's genealogy of Jesus (Luke 3:38), which traces Christ's ancestry all the way back to Adam.

Whichever interpretation may be correct, the driving thesis of this book—of Creation planned first in Heaven, followed afterwards by Creation expressed on Earth—remains valid and central to our fundamental understanding of the Creation, the Creator, and ourselves.

We are introduced to Adam in Genesis 2:7

> The Lord God formed (yatzar – long tense i.e. a continuous development that could have included an evolutionary input) the man from the dust of the ground and breathed into his nostrils the breath of life, and the man became a living being.

The word "yatzar" suggests that God modelled and fashioned Adam in the way a potter would work a piece of clay. It is another example of God using picturesque language to communicate his truths to us. We are not given a detailed description of how he formed Adam or how long he took.

Isaiah 64:8 suggests that we, too, have been made by a similar process to Adam, yet we have not been made instantaneously or literally out of a chunk of clay. It says, "You, LORD, ARE OUR FATHER. We are the clay; you are the Potter. We are *all* the work of your hand".

If slow processes were used to form humankind "in continuance", they could have correlated loosely with what Biologists term "Evolution", the main distinction being that they would have been God-guided and purposeful.

Conversely, God may have modelled and fashioned Adam from start to finish within seconds, which he certainly has the capability of doing.

Independent of these considerations is that humankind was made in two stages—in Heaven first, and then afterwards on Earth. We know neither the mechanics employed nor the timing.

Here is a verse to illustrate that humankind pre-existed in some form in Heaven before being created on Earth, even if only in the mind of God.

> Ephesians 1:4, "For he (God) chose us (believers) in him (Christ) *before the Creation of the world*".

Isn't it awesome that we were chosen *before* the world appeared in our Universe, long before the existence of Adam on our planet? We pre-existed in some mysterious sense. This becomes a key to our understanding who we *really* are.

And if Jesus Christ and his redeeming work were planned before the Earth was produced in our Cosmos, this planning must have happened in Heaven.

God knew humankind would sin against him and he made provision for our redemption before the event, even before the world appeared in our Universe.

How remarkable! How comforting!

Continuing in Genesis 2, we identify our earliest ancestors as Adam and Eve and their earliest abode being the delightful Garden of Eden. Like them, we too are prone to sin and rebellion against God, and like them, we are subject to separation from his presence.

Verses 13 and 14 reveal something especially important that is easy to miss in modern language Bible translations:

> And the Lord God commanded the man, "You are free to eat from any tree in the garden; but you must not eat from the tree of the knowledge of good and evil, for when (literally "in the *day* that) you eat of it you will surely die (literally: in dying you shall die)."

As we know from Genesis 3:6-7, Adam and Eve disobeyed, and judgement was passed on them by God. Many Christians believe this verse is teaching that all physical death entered the world only because of and at the instance of this first sin, including death for animals and even plant life; others see it as denoting animals only.

In either case, they argue, fossils could not therefore have formed prior to Adam's sin.

I do not believe this. Personally, I think death in the rest of nature pre-existed Adam's sin. For example, Adam must have had some knowledge of the meaning of death for God's warning about it to be meaningful to him. Similarly, Adam's comprehension of death must have included animals and not plant death alone for the forewarning to carry weight.

However, death in the natural world is not what "in dying you shall die" is teaching about. Far from it. It is referring to Adam's *spiritual* death. Adam continued living *physically* on Earth for hundreds of years! God would have had to be lying then if he had said to Adam that by eating the forbidden fruit he would die physically "in the day that" he did so, because he didn't! And since God does not lie, the deeper and more vital connotation of spiritual death must have been intended.

Not making allowance for the physical death of animals pre-existing Adam is holding some Christians back from accepting the geological record.

Whatever you yourself believe to be included in the consequences of Adam's sin, the concept of physical death predated sin on Earth, because we are told Jesus was the "lamb *slain before* the foundation of the world"

(Revelation 13:8). Thereby, Jesus' own earthly physical death was planned and settled before our planet appeared.

Today as we look back at Jesus' crucifixion, Christians can proclaim a reversal of the curse "in dying, you shall die". Instead we have a ringing promise that "in dying, we shall live".

Although like Adam we are subject to spiritual and physical death on Earth, we can, thanks to Jesus, embrace immortal spiritual life right now, as well as look forward with eager anticipation to living with God in the future.

Jesus confirmed this in his words recorded in John 11:25-26

> "I am the resurrection and the life. The one who believes in me will live, even though they die, and whoever lives by believing in me will never die."

Putting in the likely Times and Venues for these events helps to clarify these verses:

> I am the resurrection and the life. The one who believes in me (now, on Earth) will live even though they die (on Earth), and whoever lives (on Earth) by believing in me will never die (spiritually—living first in Paradise, then after Judgement Day will also be re-embodied and live in the New Jerusalem).

> *Believing in Jesus while on Earth ensures for us an extremely fulfilling eternal future—both physically and spiritually.*

Thousands of Christians and others who have died physically and gone to the Paradise section of Hades during a near death experience, assure us when they return that "in dying" we definitely live on!

NDErs who have enjoyed Paradise attest to the fact that there is no fear in death for Christians. A number remain uncomfortable regarding the possible circumstances involved in dying, but they nevertheless on talking to them appear to be very comfortable about death itself.

Although the Paradise section in the afterlife is only a place of waiting in spirit bodies before Judgement, the many thousands who have described it in their own words are enchanted.

Many NDErs have not had the privilege of going to the love and beauty of Paradise, but have been consigned to some section of the Prisons of Hades instead. Even so, those returnees who have applied appropriate corrections to their lives back in our world claim to have likewise learnt not to fear death.

Judgement, following Jesus' return to our world and our own bodily resurrection, will result in either our acceptance into Heaven, or sadly an existence separated eternally from God. Notice that death, as annihilation, may not be an option. Judgement and its verdict for each individual, is entirely in the hands of God. Jesus warned, "Do not judge, or you too will be judged", (Matthew 7:1). The Apostle Paul confirmed this principle when he wrote (Romans 2:1):

> You, therefore, have no excuse, you who pass judgement on someone else, for at whatever point you judge another, you are condemning yourself, because you who pass judgment do the same things.

Only God has the full picture about your life or mine, in far greater detail than we realise or remember ourselves, such that only God can judge us fairly. He even knows our "secret" thoughts.

As for me, I am eternally grateful that Jesus has already acted as my substitute for the death penalty that I deserve. I have accepted his gift of life instead.

Regardless of how much humanity might like to ignore or cheat death, it has been our companion and future since the Garden of Eden.

What is our God like, with whom we have been given the option to share eternity?

In 2010 my wife and I visited the Channel Isle of Guernsey, which had been occupied by German forces during World War 2. As the impending German invasion drew near, many children were sent off for safety to families they did not know in England, who had offered protection for the children.

Imagine you were one of those kids clutching your teddy bear and waiting amongst hundreds of other families on the docks, not knowing what lay ahead. How would you feel? What would be some of the things you would like to know about where you were headed and to whom?

Let's not be similar to those kids in trepidation on the docks. Let's learn in advance where we are going and to whom.

Learning more about our creative God and his nature, where he lives and what he is planning for when we join him, should be a priority for each of us.

The next two chapters therefore focus on the search for a fuller understanding of Father God and what he is *really* like.

CHAPTER 13

GOD SPEAKS CREATIVELY

*"By faith we understand that the Universe was formed **at God's command**, so that what is seen was not made out of what is visible."*

—Hebrews 11:3 NIV

In my studies about God, I was struck by how many similar characteristics he has to us, the humans he made. I know scripture tells us that we were designed in his likeness and image, so I should not have been as surprised as I was, but we tend to think of God as so infinite and powerful that there is a great gulf between ourselves and him. I hope to bridge that gulf in our perception.

The closer we come to the God of Creation, the deeper we can appreciate his love and purposes for us.

———⋅✳⋅———

In the third verse of the Bible, Genesis 1:3, we find our first physical revelation of God—which is as a creative voice: And God said, "Let there be light", and there was light. Our God spoke!

God's vocal commands have since played a pivotal role in the whole of Creation.

In this chapter we will contemplate the ingenuity in what God says and commands. As earlier, we will look both at scripture, and then at modern experiences that illuminate some of those scriptures.

Other scriptures besides Genesis 1 and 2 confirm the productive power of God's spoken word.

The Holman Christian Standard Bible renders Psalm 33:9 clearly: "For he spoke, and it came into being; he commanded, and it came into existence."

It is because of the authority and creativity of the voice of God in scripture, and in modern times, that the precise words he says are massively significant.

It is as a voice that we most frequently encounter almighty God in the Bible. God speaks to communicate lovingly as well as to create and command.

We alone of God's creatures on this planet echo his ability to speak lovingly and productively. This is because we "shadow" him. We may be poor and indistinct copies, but speaking with people and getting involved in helping them gives us a glimpse into what God the Father is like on a personal level.

In addition, we can study the person of Jesus because he is an exact representation of his Father, as he explained to his disciples: "Anyone who has seen me has seen the Father" (John 14:9). Jesus spoke with authority and creative power matching that of God the Father. We see his involvement in the Creation that continues until today (Hebrews 1:2-3):

> In these last days, he (God the Father) has spoken to us by his Son (Jesus), whom he appointed heir of all things, and through whom also he made the Universe. The Son is the radiance of God's glory and the exact representation of his being, sustaining all things by his *powerful word*.

Jesus was known before his incarnation on Earth as the "Word". As the Word, he played a pivotal role in Creation (John 1:1-4).

What God says is an open window into his heart and mind.

In outback Australia before the advent of modern communication, because distances are so vast, some neighbours conversed over the pedal radio for many months and even years before meeting one another face to face—and usually they felt they knew their neighbour already as a friend despite not having known what he or she looked like.

In fact, we get to know people authentically through what they say and our verbal interactions with them.

Likewise, by meditating on what God the Father has said in scripture, and through speaking with him regularly in prayer, we get to know him better. We can become closer to Jesus or to the Holy Spirit with a similar approach.

To digress quickly, what about when we address God as "Lord"? Who are we praying to? You would have to answer that for yourself, but for me I am praying to the Trinitarian One God—Father, Son and Holy Spirit as one essence, together. Otherwise I address each person of the Godhead separately—for example as "Father God" or "Lord Jesus" or "Lord Holy Spirit."

A study of God speaking in an audible voice in the Bible reveals something very surprising and ultimately edifying—we find a definite progression:

> *Initially it was God the Father who did most of the speaking with humankind: he held long conversations with Adam, Abraham, Job, Noah and Moses.

> *As history unfolded, God's representatives, the angels and prophets, and later on Jesus Christ and then the early Christians, did an increasing amount of the talking, while God the Father did less and less himself—and with increasing brevity.

Can we find a reason for this sequence? Perhaps there is a clue in the wording God used in the call of Isaiah to speak for him (Isaiah 6:8-9). At that time, Isaiah was a young man who saw God in person, and feared he would die as a consequence. God instead forgave his sins and then asked,

> "Whom shall I send? And who will go for us?"
> Isaiah answered, "Here am I. Send me."
> God responded, "Go and **tell** this people..."

We find a comparable mandate repeated when Jesus commanded the disciples, "Go into all the world and *preach* the gospel to all Creation" (Mark 16:15).

So, we find that God delegates to his representatives that they should speak for him, most specifically his warnings and his salvation message.

Speech is a gift that imitates God, thereby enabling us to function as his "shadow" on Earth—the God who speaks. This facilitates our individual and unique relationships with him.

And as we learn to speak more effectively for him, he chooses to speak to people audibly himself less and less. He is obviously training us to be his spokespersons.

In speaking to God and for God, new spiritual fruit grows within Christians. They draw closer to him and comprehend better who he is and what his plans are.

Consequently, a process that began in the Old Testament as the personal responsibility of a few chosen prophets to speak directly on behalf of God has become a corporate one. Christians nowadays are expected to fulfil that role.

An interesting question is—does scripture record Father God speaking audibly on Earth after the advent of Jesus into the world?

The answer is "yes", though it was not a frequent occurrence, and that is still the case today.

At Jesus' baptism God said, "You are my Son, whom I love; with you I am well pleased" (Luke 3:22).

In John 12:28, Jesus called out "Father, glorify your name" and God the Father responded from Heaven where he lives, "I have glorified it, and will glorify it again".

Later, on a high mountain with Peter, James and John as witnesses, God repeated his benediction of Jesus—but added the extra instruction **"Listen to him!"** (Matthew 17:5)

And Peter conversed with God in Acts10:13-15 about clean and unclean foods, which interchange was to have much significance in Peter's life the very next day.

Still today, with so many contrary voices grabbing our attention, we need to listen to God, especially the Holy Spirit during times of quiet prayer and Bible reading. His speaking with us is seldom audible, but nonetheless is a definite spiritual communication.

There are stories and testimonies of people hearing the audible voice of God in situations where on reflection they know no other voice in our world would have achieved the same impact or result.

This has been a definite spoken voice with clear words, inside or outside themselves, on occasion heard by others also.

It seems uncommon to hear God's voice more than once or twice in a lifetime.

I have for years been collecting reliable descriptions of God speaking audibly to someone on Earth, to learn more about him.

One incident was written out for me by David Craig, an Australian I met soon after I arrived in this country in the mid-1980s.

As a young man, David became an alcoholic who was seldom sober. Unable to beat his addiction, and in a drunken stupor, he decided to end his miserable life. He swallowed handfuls of pills and lay down on a rock, expecting the overdosing to kill him, or that once comatose he would be drowned by the incoming tide.

Later that night, David found himself floating in the swollen waters at the mouth of the Johnstone River in Queensland, Australia. The cool water helped revive him and he remembered that he had come there, to Flying Fish Point, specifically to commit suicide. The pills had drifted him into unconsciousness as he had planned. However, the tide must have risen such that it floated him out into the estuary.

Now that David had sobered up and the salt water had made him vomit up most of the overdose of pills, he no longer wanted to die! He struck out towards the lights blinking across the water through the darkness and drizzle.

No sooner had David struggled up the shore than he heard an authoritative voice say to him:

"David, I have more for you to do than this."

David turned around slowly and looked for the speaker, but there was no one to be seen. He was shocked. The voice had seemed to have come from all around him, from the very air. He kept peering, but it was a rainy night and people had wisely stayed indoors.

"David, I have more for you to do than this."

Those words kept reverberating inside his mind. A deep and unexplored part of David, a part ignored since childhood, told him it must be God who had spoken; but why? David had become an atheist who had spent hours in pubs arguing against the existence of God, so now he was particularly confused. He decided to stagger home and try to think it through later.

Years have passed since I first interviewed David in Brisbane in the 1980s, and he is no longer a hopeless and suicidal alcoholic. As a direct result of God speaking to him, David sought and found Christ as his personal Saviour and Lord. Jesus subsequently graciously helped him beat his addiction to alcohol.

David visited me at home in Toowoomba some years after my initial interviews with him. When I opened the door to see who had knocked, I did not recognise him at first—he looked so different—happy and healthy.

But there was more to the change in his looks than the fresh, healthy glow. When I discussed this with David later, he described a miracle healing he had had from incurable Parkinson's disease subsequent to my first meeting him. This healing had contributed to the change in his looks because Parkinson's had previously removed expression from his face.

As we spoke, I could hardly believe the positive changes I saw in David—physically, emotionally, socially and spiritually. God had continued to intervene creatively in his life on each of these levels. At that time, David was serving God as an Anglican priest, and continued to do so in various positions and countries before retiring recently in Australia. Although officially retired, he remains very active in his Christian service.

What important lessons might we glean about God from what he said aloud to David? That is our focus. God's precise wording was: "David, I have more for you to do than this."

> *He used David's name, so knew him personally, despite David being a vocal atheist and an alcoholic. During dark times, we may suppose that our sins or rejection of God to have permanently spoilt our chances of a close relationship with him, but don't you believe it! That's a lie!

> *God's words to David suggest that he has a worthwhile purpose for even the most desperate and lost person; furthermore, suicide is absolutely not part of that plan.

All individual lives, until they have run their God-ordained course, are consistently shown by him to have a meaningful future and a deepening purpose to fulfil.

You and I are no exceptions; we matter to God, who loves us as much as he loves David.

David was an atheist when he heard God speaking to him. But what of Christians, why should God need to speak aloud to them? Don't they have the scriptures and the voice of the Holy Spirit within, plus a sensitised conscience, and often Godly friends to advise them?

Yes they do, and these are far and away the most common means of communication, but on rare occasions God nevertheless speaks audibly to Christians, conceivably because the instructions are urgent, or so specific and unusual that they require special confirmation.

For example, a close friend, Vic Moore, was told audibly by God as he walked across a room at home in New Zealand to "Go to Malawi", even though Vic did not know where Malawi was and had to find it on a map. Brenda and I met Vic in Malawi when I went there as a Teacher and confirm that he was a very effective servant for God in that African nation. God knows what he is doing when selecting true servants.

A Tasmanian lady, a Christian, wrote to me about how God had told her the full name of a girl her son had made pregnant, even though she had never heard any mention of this girl previously, not even her name! It had not been a long-term or committed relationship, and her son had not married the girl, but this name spoken aloud by God to her in her kitchen enabled that lady to seek out the single mother and child. She found them and give her grandson the love and help he would not otherwise have had access to. She has loved and supported the young mother since in a variety of practical ways. Grandparents can play a significant role in God's purposes.

Once again, God's compassion and intimate knowledge of personal lives is striking. His concern would appear to include everyone, not only Christians.

Another example of a specific name being provided aloud by God was to a Methodist Minister, Rev. Frank Mussell[31], who many years ago wanted to build a retreat centre in Rhodesia (now Zimbabwe), but didn't know where to start to obtain some land:

> I remember putting my head in my hands and closing my eyes and saying audibly, "Lord, who can I ask for land?"
>
> I immediately became conscious of a Voice speaking to me, a very clear one, and it said, "Try Mr Webb".

> I recall sitting back in my chair and repeating the words "Try Mr Webb"? I asked myself, "Who is Mr Webb?"

As he pondered this strange experience, Frank Mussell remembered that he had met a Mr Webb two years earlier at a social event, but had not seen him since.

Wondering how he might trace Mr Webb, he half-remembered that his quarry might attend a Baptist church, and he found through this vague memory how to contact him. Embarrassed and unsure how to proceed, he wrote a tentative letter to Mr Webb.

Mr Milton Webb, meanwhile, unbeknown to anyone else, had "given" a beautiful little valley on his farm to God in prayer, "for whatever you decide to use it for, Lord." This secret gift to God of that beautiful valley was in gratitude for recent unexpected financial help when Milton needed it desperately.

A wonderful Christian centre, cottages and youth camp slowly developed on that land as a faith venture by Frank Mussell, who named the complex Resthaven, based on the Lord's invitation in Mark 6:31 to his overextended and exhausted disciples, who had not even had the opportunity to eat because of their busyness:

> "Come ye yourselves apart... and rest a while" (King James Bible)

Over the years, many lives have been transformed, enriched, and even rescued at Resthaven. When I took youth camps there, the centre seemed to have a special peaceful atmosphere and good things always happened.

Resthaven stands today as a monument to God's modern and continuing voice intervening creatively in our world.

What does God's voice sound like? We might anticipate his instructions to boom out loudly and with great authority. This may happen, but it is not what people have reported to me.

Some report that God's voice was male and insistent but not loud, others that it evoked a strange excitement in them, and still others report their emotions running the gamut from perplexity to joy and wonder.

Although not all hearers recognised at first that it was God speaking to them, all soon did so. It appears that there is an intuitive comprehension that it is God speaking even when he is addressing an atheist such as David Craig.

The fact that God speaks aloud to atheists, addicts and criminals more frequently than to Christians, illustrates that hearing his audible voice is not a reward for holiness or Christian maturity.

Nor is asking him to speak to us a substitute for reading and obeying scripture, nor for listening to the frequent, gentle, inner promptings of the Holy Spirit.

The structure of what God says and the way he says it is revealing. He often gives a short instruction, maybe twice, on rare occasions three times, using the same or similar words. However, he does not nowadays appear to enter into conversation or debate with persons on Earth any more than he did in New Testament times. The experiences of people in the early years of the church and in our modern-day mesh very closely.

Hundreds of written reports by returnees from an NDE report having had conversations with Father God in the afterlife, most commonly during a searching Life Review.

Many NDErs can at first be in awe or fear on meeting God in the afterlife. They may bow in reverence to him. The love of God streaming outwards from him and the words he says quickly calms the NDEr. Others report no initial fear on meeting God the Father such as we might have on our planet, in part because of this signature love that beams in advance towards them in some enigmatic fashion.

Subsequently, the NDEr may have a personal conversation with God, occasionally a long one, during which God answers questions patiently as a father might be expected to do.

God is awesome, powerful and authoritative, but very personable and sociable too. Many NDErs report how uplifted they felt after conversing with him. These conversations have customarily proved life-changing when once again picking up the threads of life on Earth.

NDErs have discovered during their Life Reviews that the things they said previously while in the world sometimes had far-reaching repercussions of which they were not aware. Our words can have ripple effects amongst others and scripture warns us to be careful what we say. Jesus established this principle in Matthew 12:34-37

> The mouth speaks what the heart is full of. A good man brings good things out of the good stored up in him, and an evil man brings evil things out of the evil stored up in him.
>
> But I tell you that everyone will have to give account on the Day of Judgment for every empty word they have spoken. For by your words you will be acquitted, and by your words you will be condemned.

Suppose someone tells you they have heard God speak to them, or you yourself are unsure whether you have genuinely heard God speaking to you in an audible voice. We need to be cautious: mental institutions often contain some patients who believe falsely that God has spoken to them. In addition, certain brain conditions and drug states can induce internal "voices" that are nothing to do with God, as can different forms of spiritism.

When God has genuinely spoken, a feeling of peace follows, without fear or agitation. Nor does God speak to endorse or encourage sin; for example, a "message" that you could start an adulterous affair would not be coming from God but from your enemy.

If you are still not sure about the source of a "voice" after applying the above checks, the incident should be discussed with a Christian Minister or Pastor. Make some enquiries first to find a person experienced in such things.

What will Father God look like when we first see him? Scripture and modern experience both demonstrate that the Father can speak with an audible voice, but does he have a mouth like we do? Does he have feelings like we have?

We had better investigate more deeply what God is *truly* like, because we who have accepted his offer of forgiveness are going to spend eternity with him.

It is almost impossible to comprehend God's creativity in our lives, or his plans and our place within them, unless we see clearly first who he is.

As we look at more scriptural revelations and some further descriptions about God's person, we could be in for a few surprises.

CHAPTER 14

QUALITIES OF GOD

"The Universe is centred on neither the Earth nor the sun. It is centred on God."

—Alfred Noyes[32]

Just as society has discovered it valuable to have a profile of a person and their background in order more fully to appreciate their actions, for example a musician and his music, or an artist and his emotive paintings, so it is with God—our comprehension of his Creation and who we *really* are will both be enhanced if we probe who he is—his physical presence, intellect, nature and past involvement.

At some period in our lives we look around us and wonder *why* the Creation happened at all, *why* humankind exists, and *why* the world is as we find it.

So, let's profile God the Creator, and hope that who God *actually* is emerges, and thereby who we are by association.

THE LIGHT OF GOD DURING BIBLICAL ENCOUNTERS

What will you see first when you come into the physical presence of God the Father, or of his son Jesus Christ? Have you ever wondered about this?

Most likely, you will first experience a glorious light. Several scripture verses specify that God lives in light. We know God "wraps himself in light as with a garment"? (Psalm 104:2). God himself, we are told in 1Timothy 6:16, "lives in unapproachable light", in Heaven.

Thousands of NDErs in their spirit bodies have met with God, many face to face, without suffering any personal damage. Despite its intensity, his light does not hurt the eyes in the afterlife; such a bright light on Earth would have damaged the retina. That is because the light is not sensed with eyes in the afterlife, but it appears to be "seen" directly by the soul in the spirit body. Most discover very quickly that although God might shine like "a hundred thousand suns" in the afterlife, there is no danger in looking directly at him.

Even on Earth, light is still fundamentally a mystery to Physics. We know much about it, its composition and its behaviour, but what it is fundamentally remains problematic. This is partly because of its dual nature, as both wave and particle, but more fundamentally because it is an energy, and we still don't know exactly what that means. We know lots about what energies do, but little about what they are and whence they originally came.

Manifestations of a glorious light before God speaks are recorded in the Bible: Isaiah, Moses, Ezekiel and others had such experiences. Moses was hidden in the cleft of a rock, in the shadows, such that the glorious light of God did not harm him as God passed by (Exodus 33:22-23).

God has produced some mysterious effects with light and its opposite, darkness, on our planet. When Christ died at noon, a deep darkness fell; this was not explicable as an eclipse because its coverage was far wider, longer (3 hours), and occurred at the new moon (Passover Time), and a solar eclipse occurs only when the moon is full. Ancient historians Phegon, Thallus and Africanus mentioned the event, but outside of scripture (Mark 15:33), these historical accounts lack detail. Earlier in history, during the plagues in Egypt, God made selected areas dark and others light—independent of the sun (Exodus 10:21-23).

Let's go back to God's designing the Cosmos. God determined that light was to be a part of our Universe; it became a feature of himself for us to live in, preparing us for a future life spent with him, because God *is* Light (1John 1:5). He not only lives in light, and shines with light: he *is* light, yet is too vast and mysterious for us to grasp comprehensively who he is—consequently, it is no wonder that we in our limited Cosmos cannot grasp fully what light *really* is.

THE LIGHT OF GOD DURING EARTHLY ENCOUNTERS

Most people have heard of Alcoholics Anonymous and the great work they do, but fewer know how it started. So… how and why did it start? Bill Wilson, the co-founder, explains its origins in *Alcoholics Anonymous Comes of Age*.

Bill Wilson describes how he lay dying in hospital from alcoholism and called out "If there is a God, let Him show Himself! I am ready to do anything, anything!"

> Suddenly the room lit up with a great white light. I was caught up into an ecstasy which there are no words to describe. It seemed to me, in my mind's eye, that I was on a mountain and that a wind not of air but of spirit was blowing. And then it burst upon me that I was a free man!
>
> Slowly the ecstasy subsided.
>
> I lay on the bed, but now for a time I was in another world, a new world of consciousness. All about me and through me there was a wonderful feeling of Presence, and I thought to myself, "So this is the God of the preachers!"

Bill got out of bed determined never to touch another drop of alcohol. This involved a tremendous struggle that was assisted by the support of a Doctor he met, who was also an alcoholic. Between them they devised a twelve-step program to sobriety that is still used by AA worldwide. The first steps on this are to admit you cannot help yourself and that you need the help of God, the same God whose presence had filled Bill's hospital room with light.

Both Bill and the Doctor remained sober, and AA has helped millions to escape from alcohol dependence.

It is interesting that hundreds of other desperate alcoholics have also reported sublime experiences of meeting with God personally, as Bill Wilson did. Nevertheless, the greater majority of alcoholics do not experience God's light and presence in this miraculous way, though many will testify to the help and intervention of God as they seek freedom from their addiction.

Dexter Froude[33] had been a despairing alcoholic before God rescued him. He provided his account to me in the late 1980s—wanting me to describe it in articles or a book for the benefit of others, which I have done previously.

Dexter describes a similar experience to Bill Wilson's, and how the bright light was accompanied by "electricity running through my body". At first, he sank back on the bed, terrified, eyes wide open, expecting to be destroyed. All his past sins began to parade through his mind and he believed that he was heading towards that Hell he had heard about as a child. Furthermore, he understood that this was no less than he deserved.

Just as suddenly as it began for Dexter, the experience stopped and the light faded.

Where was he? In Hell already? Tentatively, he stretched out a hand towards the bedroom wall and felt a flood of relief when he touched it. He was alive! But his new perception of his sin had him calling out in anguish, "God, why am I alive? Why didn't you destroy me?"

A deep, authoritative voice replied, "Dexter, I want you to tell others of my grace. Preach the gospel and heal the sick."

Overcome with emotion, tears streaming down his face, Dexter managed to respond, "Yes, Lord. Yes, Lord." He leapt out of bed and poured his remaining whiskey down the hotel washbasin. His desire for alcohol left him that night.

What happened next illustrates how God deals with us personally as individuals. At that time, Dexter was illiterate. However, a great and inexplicable desire arose in him to read the Bible. He bought a Bible, opened it and gazed in frustration at the meaningless jumble of letters on the pages. A picture arose in his mind of what the Bible was saying. As his eyes travelled over the pages, the vision changed. He describes what he saw like being at the movies.

God taught Dexter over many weeks to read by supplying dynamic pictorial visions like this of what the Bible was portraying!

Once he could read adequately, Dexter's visions stopped.

From that time and until I met him some years later, Dexter had been a faithful and effective servant of God.

Dexter Froude and Bill Wilson were not Christians when they experienced God's light and their lives were turned around. But what about Christians?

Daniel Kawata, a prominent and dynamic Christian in Zaire (the Congo), experienced a "huge light in my office and a voice saying 'Everything you have belongs to you, but you belong to Me. You need to join World Vision. It won't be easy for you. Zaire will be in great turmoil, but I will be with you'."

Daniel subsequently became Field Director for World Vision in turbulent Zaire. As promised, God has been was him and the staff in the World Vision office throughout the rioting, murder and mayhem. His life has been spared miraculously on a number of occasions.

The memory of that beautiful light in his office and spoken promise gave Daniel the strength to cope. His very effective ministry for God continues.

In the majority of accounts, the light of God seen on Earth evokes awe not fear. It is described as transmitting love, comfort and even healing—which are similar descriptions to those given by NDErs when encountering God's light for the first time in the afterlife.

In some inexplicable manner, God's light seems to transmit his very essence, at least to some degree. Might that be related to the unexpected revelation in 1John 1:5 that God *IS* light?

SEEING GOD

At this point, we may wonder about the verse in Exodus 33:20 when God said to Moses, "You cannot see my face, for no one may see me and live."

The meaning and context of God's statement are important. He was referring to this specific encounter, for earlier in verse 11 of the same chapter we read: "The Lord would speak to Moses *face to face*, as one speaks to a friend". When you talk face to face with friends, you certainly see their faces. Descriptions in scripture show that others besides Moses spoke with the Lord "face to face", yet lived.

The light around God can vary in intensity; Moses had basically asked to see all of it, "his glory". The context suggests that it was the intensity of God's glorious energy that would have been too great for Moses while on Earth to survive.

The Israelites from Moses' era forward became terrified of any encounter with God in case it was in circumstances where all of God's glory was being manifested, in which case they would have been destroyed, and how could they tell in advance? But on one occasion, more than seventy men saw God at one time and were not destroyed (Exodus 24:9-11).

Statements about God as one whom "no one has seen or can see" (1Timothy 6:16), and Jesus' words "No one has seen the Father except the one who is from God, only he has seen the Father" (John 6:46), are referring to seeing God in his fullness and his glory, because lots of people in the Bible had already seen God and lived.

Jesus, however, was unique; he alone at that time had seen God in the totality that Moses, Isaiah, Jacob and others could not without dying.

God Is Spirit

Does God ever manifest in our world as a man? After all, the Bible teaches in John 4:24 that "God is spirit, and his worshipers must worship in the Spirit and in truth". This is so, but the verse is not saying God has no other characteristics or presentation—in other scriptures we learn that God *is* light (but he is not only light); and that God *is* love (but he is not only love) and so on.

The verse "God *is* spirit" can be likened to a statement about humankind: "Humans are intelligent and should worship in an intelligent way". This statement would not mean that we are intelligence alone—no body, no emotions, no personality, no character, no spirit, no social dimension, no musical ability—only intelligence. Similarly, God is not limited to being "spirit" alone. He is revealed most commonly in scripture as having a body, emotions, an intellect, an inventive nature and a social dimension, amongst other features and qualities such as love, light, absolute power, knowledge and wisdom.

Despite the detailed revelation of God in the Bible to the contrary, many Christians have a sort of "spirit only" concept of God the Father; that he exists all around us like the air, but concurrently in Heaven. This may be partially true, but it is not by any means everything that the Bible reveals about him.

It may surprise you, but God the Father and Jesus are usually portrayed in scripture as active men.

The Holy Spirit, God's own spirit, is not portrayed as a man but as a dove, or fire, or oil, or the wind—a Spirit pervasive throughout the surface of the Earth, yet one in nature with God in Heaven.

Scripture is clear that God the Father and Jesus can appear physically as men at any point in history, whereas it is God the Holy Spirit who remains in our world as their usually invisible divine representative and presence.

It is interesting that hundreds of NDErs have described interactions with Father God or with Jesus, both of whom are described as appearing to the NDErs in the form of a man. No prolonged NDE description that I have read has given a comprehensive description of meeting God as a spirit alone; nor, incidentally, as a woman.

The Holy Spirit, the third person of the Trinity, is not generally mentioned in NDEs. His separate involvement with us would appear to be in the main on Earth.

The Father or the Son sometimes choose to enter the world in a recognisable, physical form, but they generally leave their ongoing creative work on Earth to the invisible Holy Spirit—and to followers of Christ.

LIKE FATHER LIKE SON—IN PHYSICAL BODIES

The human body is the form in which the Son of God, Jesus Christ, lived in our world "made in human likeness" (Philippians 2:7), while still being in the nature of God (Philippians 2:6), so it is not surprising that God in

Heaven may be seen in bodily form as a man by us too—if he so chooses. Like Son, like Father.

NDErs confirm such observations, including some who were previously atheists or agnostics—they have asserted that they interacted with God the Father in the likeness of a man. Some, such as Angie Fenimore[34], describe meeting with both God the Father and with Jesus at the same time, both apparently in the bodily form of men.

Here is another description of Father and Son being together, written by Erica P[35]:

> Then I left the room and was traveling down a tunnel with a bright light. As I went further up the tunnel, the light got bigger and brighter. Then I was in the throne room of God. Jesus Christ was seated next to God. The throne room was pure white. Then I stood there in absolute awe at the beauty of Jesus. Jesus was wearing a white robe with a purple sash.... Then I remember bowing before Jesus and God. They both spoke to me, but I do not remember what was said by them.

Our conclusion is that Father God at this time chooses to live in bodily form in Heaven, at least some of the time, akin to both his Son and humankind. Of course, his body and that of Jesus are immortal while our present bodies are mortal, although our resurrection bodies will be immortal like theirs (1Corinthians 15:53-54). And at times he speaks as we do. Consider his self-declaration in Psalm 89:34 "I will not alter what my *lips* have uttered". Jesus appeared to confirm God speaking like us in Matthew 4:4 when quoting the Old Testament to the devil: "Man shall not live on bread alone, but on every word that comes from the *mouth* of God."

Even during earthly appearances when he may be shining with his glorious light, God will present or allude to himself with the physical attributes of a man. Consider again his appearance to Moses (Exodus 33:22-23):

> When my glory passes by, I will put you in a cleft in the rock and cover you with *my hand* until I have passed by. Then I will remove my hand and you will see *my back*; but *my face* must not be seen.

There is certainly much more to God the Father than human likeness, just as there was more to his glory than Moses could experience on our planet and survive.

However, we can only relate to Father God as he presents himself to us, which, in most cases in scripture, on Earth in recent times, and during NDEs, is as a man. This is certainly a true representation because it is how God has chosen to reveal himself.

Like Father like Son.

Like Son, like Father.

And why do we occupy similar physical bodies, you may wonder? And what does this suggest to us?

God in Visions

Many of the scriptural encounters with God written about, such as those of Adam and Eve, Abraham and Sarah, Isaiah, Jacob and Moses, are interactions with God in a physical form.

The visions of God found in Revelation, Daniel, Ezekiel and elsewhere are not God's tangible appearances, but are more like dreams. While visions add to our concept of who God is, each is unreliable as a description of what God is like bodily. Visions and dreams express concepts rather than physical accuracy and there is a substantial difference between information imparted in visions and dreams from that communicated face to face. God himself makes this distinction forcefully and clarifies the point in Numbers 12:6-9

> *Listen to my words:*
> "When there is a prophet among you,
> I, the Lord, reveal myself to them in visions,
> I speak to them *in dreams.*
> *But this is not true of my servant Moses*;
> he is faithful in all my house.
> With him I speak *face to face,*
> clearly, and not in riddles;
> he sees the *form* of the Lord."

Therefore, in Heaven, you may expect to see God face to face, and relate to him as to a man in physical form, as Moses did, and many others have done in more recent times during NDEs.

DIVINE INTELLECT AND CREATIVITY

We realise God has intellectual, emotional, social and character attributes superior but similar to our own, created as we have been to be like him.

To perceive and appreciate God's work in creating us and the world we live in, we need to briefly familiarise ourselves with these characteristics.

Scripture reveals that all around us in nature is the evidence whereby we can come to know and appreciate God's invisible power and intellect. People who pray and meditate in beautiful natural surroundings can find a closeness to God that is difficult to enjoy in the bustle and stress of city life.

His originality and life force permeate all of his Creation:

> For since the Creation of the world God's *invisible qualities*—his eternal *power* and *divine nature*—have been clearly seen, being understood from what has been made, so that people are without excuse. (Romans 1:20)

This is a fascinating verse. What we see expressed in the created world helps us to understand our invisible God better, especially his creative power and nature.

An awesome intelligence must be behind the design of the tiny atom—as well as the design of the vast Cosmos. There are ongoing laws which govern them, that illustrate God's extraordinary capabilities and divine intellect. I am sure all monotheistic religions and certainly all true Christians recognise this.

God's innovative genius is startling and constantly on view in our Cosmos, but interpretations of its significance can vary. I am reminded of a public meeting that I organised in Malawi for a visiting astronomer, who showed colour slides and spoke enthusiastically about the wonders of the Universe. At the close of the meeting a young woman approached me.

"I found the sizes and distances he spoke about overwhelming. I can't believe that God cares for little me as just another person amongst billions of others on this tiny planet."

"That's so interesting," I responded, "because I had the opposite reaction. The fact that I can see such careful design on such a large scale excites me, and assures me that I can trust God for my tiny life. I find it comforting that he is big enough and smart enough to do all that."

We had been given the same information but had opposite reactions to it.

I don't think what I said impressed her because I did not notice her at any other Christian meetings.

On thinking back over our interaction, I decided it is not what we see that convinces us about God, it is how we interpret what we see. She and I saw the same slides and heard the same lecture—in my heart I said '"Wow", while she was responding, "God is too big to care about little me."

Indeed, God knows today our "secret" thoughts and plans (Psalm 94:11) and even the number of hairs on our heads (Luke 12:7). Nevertheless, despite his intimate and comprehensive knowledge of each one of us, and our failings, God still loves us. He loves that lady, he loves me, and he loves you.

"As the heavens are higher than the Earth, so are my ways higher than your ways and my thoughts than your thoughts" (Isaiah 55:9).

You and I are included in God's off-the-scale intellectual activity. His knowledge of us is personal and current, conceivably because the Holy Spirit permeates all of life.

God's consideration for us is extraordinary and meticulous: "How amazing are your thoughts concerning me, God, how vast is the sum of them. Were I to count them, they would outnumber the grains of sand" (Psalm 139:17,18).

God discloses his thoughts and plans to us in a revelatory process rather than a didactic one: he "*reveals* his thoughts to humankind" (Amos 4:13).

The truly substantial truths about God and ourselves must come to us primarily by revelation, because our logic is limited and prescribed, unable to cope successfully with issues outside our parameters.

God's Emotional Life

The Bible teaches that "God is Love" (1John 4:8), and the central message of the gospel of our salvation is predicated by this (John 3:16).

We all know that love involves, among much else, very powerful emotions.

We mirror our Father in having powerful emotions.

I will italicise God's emotions as stated in various scriptures below, to draw attention to them:

> God "feels" certain things intensely—we read of his *anger burning* (Isaiah 5:25) and in Genesis 6:6 that "The Lord regretted that he had made human beings on the Earth, and *his heart was deeply troubled*".
>
> Later in Isaiah we read statements about God such as "the Lord *longs* to be gracious to you; therefore, he will rise up to show you *compassion*". (Isaiah 30:18).

Thankfully, scripture reveals that God's compassion can in time overcome his anger, as demonstrated in Isaiah 54:7,8—God speaking:

> "For a brief moment I abandoned you,
> but with *deep compassion* I will bring you back.
> In a *surge of anger*
> I hid my face from you for a moment,
> but with *everlasting kindness*
> *I will have compassion on you*,"
> says the Lord your Redeemer.

This triumph of God's compassion over his anger underpins our hopes for our future.

Living as believers reveals that while Father God does not usually extricate us from difficult physical situations, he nevertheless empathises and sustains us in love as we go through them—as he did for Jesus' sufferings on the cross.

We are emotional beings, and so is God. That he can react emotionally makes him more accessible to us, and us to him. We know we can be understood by him.

For example, Zephaniah 3:17 reads "He will take great delight in you, in his love he will no longer rebuke you, he will rejoice over you with singing". This "rejoice" in Hebrew is the word "guwl", which means to "spin around under a strong emotion".

Can you picture God doing that? Spinning around in delight, and singing over you for something significant that you have done, such as choosing to become one of his followers? That heart response would be more expected of King David than God, which is why David was identified by God as "a man after my own heart" (Acts 13:22). Although it is a paraphrase rather than a direct translation, I like the way the Message Bible expresses God's comment: "He's a man whose heart beats to my heart".

Indeed, David's effusive, expansive, demonstrative responses shadow those of God, who is not a cold, white, marble figure sitting imperiously on a giant throne as some may envisage him; on the contrary, he is more like us—emotional, accessible, loving, and wanting to be loved.

It is more accurate to say that we are more like him.

Are you perceiving from this who you *really* are, and even why?

Returning briefly to the importance to appreciating God in nature.

Entrusting ourselves to God when converting to Christ is a helpful precursor to comprehending things in their true spiritual context, including the Creation and its continuation today as a "God thing". This explains why knowing God more closely increases our delight in nature and appreciation of his precious pinnacle of Creation—people—including ourselves.

I have noticed that conversion is frequently followed by a person's fresh wonder at the beauties of nature, and a greater and growing love both for God and for people. I heard recently of a new Christian who kept asking her husband during a journey to stop the car so that she could wonder at the beautiful views that she had not noticed previously, despite having driven along the same road many times beforehand.

THE CHARACTER OF GOD

To comprehend God's Creation and thereby know him better, we move on to the revelation of his overall character.

Originally a "charakter" was the name given to any engraving instrument e.g. a seal, by which a man's identification could be determined—a seal with his personal imprint would identify what belonged to a king. Later, it came to mean that distinguishing mark itself made on the wax, clay or stone. Subsequently it passed into our language meaning the distinguishing marks cut into the nature of a person.

Personality is related to what we show externally to the world; character is related to our inner nature. Aspects of the presentation of our personality can change depending on who we are with, but our character is more foundational, and changes slowly if at all.

God's fundamental character is known well amongst Christians—he is morally pure and righteous, holy, fair, kind, patient, generous, loving, truthful and faithful.

While we see these characteristics in people to a limited degree, God is different because he is also sinless perfection. In other words, his character is far enhanced (inadequate though that word is) in every respect to that of any good people we may know, although in them we can catch a glimpse or "shadow" of what God is like in that dimension.

This applies to Christians, Hindus, Buddhists, Muslims and people following no particular faith—they are all made in the image of God and can display that image to some degree, although sin defaces it.

> *C.C. Lewis wrote in The Great Divorce: "There is but one good; that is God. Everything else is good when it looks to Him and bad when it turns from Him."*

Christianity has a great advantage over other religions in that God offers not only a pardon for sin, but power over it, providing we become born again spiritually, as Jesus taught Nicodemus (John 3:16). Then the gentle Holy Spirit takes up invisible residence in us by invitation: and teaches, guides and helps us throughout life.

1 Corinthians 6:19 makes this clear to believers:

> Do you not know that your bodies are temples of the Holy Spirit, who is in you, whom you have received from God? You are not your own.

The Holy Spirit acts as a small, quiet voice within us, over and above our natural conscience. Although this voice is easily swamped, suppressed or ignored in our frenetic lives, his intention is for us to listen and grow the distinctive "Fruit of the Holy Spirit", as itemised in Galatians 5:22-23 (ESV)

> But the fruit of the Spirit is love, joy, peace, patience, kindness, goodness, faithfulness, gentleness and self-control. Against such things there is no law.

We see each of these "fruit" portrayed fully in Jesus' life and character on Earth.

In this way, God expresses his intention for us to grow Jesus' attributes within ourselves, by living in cooperation with the Holy Spirit.

Arrogance, unforgiveness, immorality and greed amongst other human weaknesses prevents the Holy Spirit growing Christ's nature in us.

But even if we co-operate, does God the Father have a longer-term plan than just yielding a crop of nicer people leading happier lives?

He certainly has momentous plans for us! Absolutely!

What we have done is no more than to catch a glimpse of God in this brief study, that he shines with light and love, and that we can appreciate some things about him—e.g. his physical, intellectual, emotional, character, creative and social attributes.

Even thinking of him in these few respects helps us to know God better, which in turn should lead us to loving him more, seeking him more, and increasing our appreciation of his Creation.

The wonder is that Father God becomes personally involved in our lives—right here, right now—when invited, and when we have asked for the saving work of Jesus to remove any barriers between ourselves and him.

Now that you know better *who* God *is*, the final question addressed in this book becomes **"what could be my destiny with this God?"**

PART 6

YOUR PERSONAL

DESTINY

CHAPTER 15

GOD IN OUR AFTERLIFE EXPERIENCES

In the investigation of the largest collection of near-death experiences to date, we see overwhelming evidence of God.

—Dr Jeffrey Long, on NDERF website

NDErs by the thousand consistently portray God as streaming out love and light from himself. While visiting Paradise, they are aware they are surrounded by God's vibrant, created and unique beauty there. They tell us about his deep personal knowledge of them and interest, his communication, and their ability to relate to him as a person.

When they return to life on our planet, they commonly see themselves as people with a God-given purpose.

None of this is too surprising to those of us who see revealed in the Bible the nature and character of God: his Creation, his desire to relate to us, and his preparation of an amazing future after death for those who choose life with him, as was intimated in the last chapter.

Whether or not they are already people of faith, or know anything of the Bible, NDErs visiting Paradise are amazed and thrilled to experience him in stunning locations.

God Is Love

We have discussed this already. It is the first and most striking attribute of God in which NDErs bask. It is time for an example.

Empathising with others is a vital component of love. Here is an NDE report from Mindy B[36] that illustrates God the Father's empathy. Finding problems in her marriage, Mindy chose to embrace anorexia, which subsequently led to her physical degradation, death, and her NDE.

God the Father led Mindy through her Life Review.

> I started seeing images roll in front of my eyes like a movie. With each image I saw it with pure love. I saw it through God's eyes, not my own. I knew why everything that had happened to me had happened. All of the abuse, rejection, hate, anger, abandonment. All of it had indeed meant something. God wept with me at one point. I felt more love than humanly possible.

On return to our world, Mindy recovered her health. "My husband and I are still together, and we are moving forward in amazing ways."

Here is another insight into God's love, which is always centred in others. God told NDEr Laura[37] that love was the only thing she would have to bring back to Paradise with her after she had returned to Earth, but that it was a certain kind of love, "The love I gave away."

This revelation to Laura is important for us too. Only an active love involved with God and with others, "the love we give away", will develop love in the deepest recesses of our own character, and embed it there for eternity. Self-love, however, is a well-known hindrance to personal development. Unfortunately, much of the popular media, of "modern" education, and almost all advertising, is aimed squarely at self-love rather than loving others and developing the communities around us.

God Is Light

NDErs by the thousand confirm that a heavenly light pours out from God the Father. It is almost as if that light imparts the essence of God himself.

Here is how Crystal McVea[38] described that light:

> It wasn't just a light –or at least not light as we know it. It was closest to the colour we call white, but a trillion times whiter than the whitest white you've ever seen or could imagine.
>
> It was brilliant and beaming and beautifully illuminating, and that's why I call it a "brightness" …
>
> But there was another dimension to it. There was also the sensation of cleanliness. It was a feeling of absolute purity and perfection, of something completely unblemished and unbroken, and being immersed in it filled me with the kind of peace and assurance I'd never known on Earth. It was like being bathed in love. It was a brightness I didn't just see but felt.

This feature of the light transmitting love and peace, mentioned by numerous NDErs, makes it especially mysterious. How can God's light transmit his nature and emotions?

Captain Dale Black[39] made some acute observations during his NDE, as one might expect a highly trained and intelligent airline pilot to make.

> Somehow, I knew that light and life and love were connected and interrelated.
>
> It was as if the very heart of God lay open for everyone in Heaven to bask in its glory, to warm themselves in its presence, to bathe in its almost liquid properties, so they could be restored, renewed and refreshed.
>
> Remarkably, the light didn't shine on things but through them. Through the grass. Through the trees. Through the wall. And through the people who were gathered there.

PMH Atwater[40], a bold and perceptive researcher of NDEs, has interviewed hundreds of returnees in a search to find out more and thereby understand her own three NDEs better. I respect her search and research, although my own analysis and conclusions differ from hers. She records a description given to her by Robin Michelle Halberdier:

> "My first visual memory was looking forward and seeing a brilliant bright light, almost like looking directly at the sun. The strange thing was that I could see my feet in front of me, as if I were floating upward in a vertical position. I do not remember passing through a tunnel or anything like that, just floating in the beautiful light. A tremendous amount of warmth and love came from the light."

Robin was just *one month old* when she had this NDE. Only much later, once she could talk, could she tell her parents about it.

Light and love are part of God's essence, and NDErs of all faiths or none who meet with him in the afterlife have recorded this extraordinary meld.

Often, an NDEr's first indication of God is the approach of a brilliant light.

Please imagine you are in Paradise and facing this light that appears to be as bright as many suns, yet does not hurt your eyes. You become enveloped by a loving, warm radiance emanating from it. Once you have adjusted, what might you notice next? Here is a typical quote taken from just one returnee's descriptions:

> Robin Michelle Halberdier[41]: "There was a standing figure in the light, shaped like a normal human being, but with no distinct facial features. It had a masculine presence.
>
> The light I have described seemed like it emanated from that figure. Light rays shone all around him. I felt very protected and safe and loved.

The figure in the light told me through what I now know to be mental telepathy that I must go back, that it was not time for me to come here.

I wanted to stay because I felt so full of joy and so peaceful.

The voice repeated that it wasn't my time; I had a purpose to fulfil and I could come back after I completed it.

God Communicates

God invariably communicates telepathically in the afterlife, confirmed worldwide in thousands of written reports.

Telepathy does not depend on ponderous air vibrations and ears and brain function, but utilises rapid communication directly into the person's soul. Kimberly Clark-Sharp[42] describes this:

> The Light gave me knowledge, though I heard no words. We did not communicate in English or in any other language. This was discourse clearer and easier than the clumsy medium of language. It was something like understanding math or music—nonverbal knowledge, but knowledge no less profound.
>
> I was learning the answers to the eternal questions of life—questions so old we laugh them off as clichés.
>
> Why are we here?
>
> "To learn."
>
> What's the purpose of our life?
>
> "To love."
>
> I felt as if I was re-remembering things I had once known but somehow forgotten, and it seemed incredible that I had not figured out these things before now.

Jesus explained this use of telepathy in Paradise to a very new arrival—Laura M[43]:

> He spoke to me, telling me that it was not my time and that I needed to return to my body, to complete my life's mission.

I did not respond to His remark, but instead asked Him how he had done that?? Spoken to me without words, without a voice, yet I had clearly heard and understood every unspoken word??

He said to me that I was in a different "place", one in which communication was purely exchanged, through the Language of Love. Here everyone spoke heart-to-heart and soul-to-soul, so that there could never be a misunderstanding.

When I had been on Earth and used the spoken word, often there had been great confusions—as what I thought I said and what was heard by my listener were often very different.

Pegi R[44] was one of a tiny number of NDErs who definitely did not want to stay in Paradise, because of wanting to return to her needy sons. She intended to make that very plain to God, who was seated and looking intently at her.

God spoke to me, and I replied to him.

I was rude and disrespectful. I started screaming that I didn't want to be there and didn't want to stay. I was very angry. I told him I have young sons at home that need me. I screamed, "I won't stay!"

Then God let me know, through thought (telepathy), that I may be trying to get my way, but that I was not the boss there.

So… I humbled myself before him, and asked him to look into the future, and I said, "If my sons would be better off without me, I will agree to stay." If they wouldn't be, I begged to go back to take care of them.

Then I saw them, my sons at home, being raised by their dad without me there. They were so sad and alone. He had a girlfriend and she didn't love them the way I loved them, and they missed me terribly.

I was so sad and I longed to comfort them.

I then asked God, "Who else will teach them about you?"

Suddenly I was back in the wheelchair, entering my body.

GOD KNOWS US

A personal Life Review features in many accounts by NDErs. That God has preserved all the precise information about people that is shown to them during the replay of their lives is awesome. During it, important events from that person's overall life history, the things they had chosen to do or think while on Earth, is reviewed—not as a Judgement, but as an opportunity for self-evaluation.

Some older children and adults report Life Reviews running chronologically, from the womb to the moment of death, while others are shown their lives as one overall 3D presentation simultaneously in some mysterious way: the spirit and soul once freed from the ponderous brain seems able to absorb masses of information almost instantaneously.

Considering the individuality of Life Reviews, we perceive part of a great principle, that during NDEs God communicates with people in a way they comprehend best. The review is succinct and never inaccurate or confusing.

These comprehensive reviews illustrate that our lives on Earth matter to God, in particular the choices we make.

Time to consider some examples.

God often begins by asking the NDEr briefly what they have done with their life, followed by an incredibly fast yet detailed visual run through of their lives to that point, generally in 3D and full colour, in which they see a selection of significant or even seemingly trivial events replayed.

Ricky Randolph[45] describes his Life Review:

> I held my hands up in front of me and could make out the appearance of a figure sitting on some type of seat.
> Then without warning it happened.
> "What have you done with your life?"
> The voice penetrated my very being. I had no answer.
> Then to my right I saw what seemed to be like a movie, and I was in it. I saw my mother giving me birth, my childhood, and friends. I

saw everything from my youth up. I saw everything I had ever done before my eyes.

All interviewees, including atheists, instinctively know that there is no point in trying to dissemble or hide anything from God, who they realise knows everything about them anyway. This intimate knowledge is what might be expected of an omniscient God, but goes far beyond what the interviewee might have anticipated. It includes things the NDEr had considered private and which can shock them as they are revealed. God generally remains supportive, like a loving Father who has been watching his child even though he is not pleased at certain things that had been done, said or thought.

The Life Review is regularly described as "gruelling", showing scenes from the person's life that he or she had hoped no-one knew about stretching back to babyhood—including inappropriate, mean, immoral or downright evil things that had been done.

God seldom interrupts. However, if the NDEr wants to bail out, God instructs him or her to keep looking, and to their surprise they still sense love not loathing coming from him. And if something confuses them, God may quickly explain why it has been included, as a good Father or Teacher might.

Actions that may have appeared unimportant to the NDEr can be included, good or bad, giving evidence that God evaluates things differently to how we do. Ricky Randolph[46] provides an example:

> I saw a man in his car that had run out of gas. I had stopped and given him a lift to a local store about a year ago. I had bought him some gas as he had no money and helped him get on his way.
>
> I thought to myself, "why am I seeing this?"
>
> The voice was loud and clear.
>
> "You took no thought to help this soul and asked nothing in return. These actions are the essence of good."

NDErs are shown forgotten details and even unknown ones in their Life Review. For example, some have reported seeing their mother in it for the very first time, since their mother had died giving birth to them.

There is a ripple effect from things we do in the world which we cannot know about or even envisage fully unless revealed, which happens to many NDErs.

The ripple effect from loving or thoughtful actions can have very positive outcomes, but negative actions can do the reverse. Here are a couple of examples to illustrate this flow. The first is written by Alexa[47]:

> My Life Review began. I was given to understand that that was what it was. This was awful.
>
> EVERYTHING (her capitals) I ever thought, did, said, hated, helped, did not help, should have helped, was shown in front of me, to the crowd of hundreds and everyone—like a movie. How mean I'd been to people, how I could have helped them, how mean I was (unintentionally also) to animals. Yes. Even the animals had had feelings.
>
> It was horrible. I fell on my face in shame. I saw how my acting, or not acting, rippled in effect towards other people and their lives.
>
> It wasn't until then that I understood how each little decision or choice affects the World.
>
> The sense of letting my Saviour down was too real.
>
> Strangely, even during this horror, I felt a compassion, an acceptance of my limitations, by Jesus and the crowd of others.

The Muslim man Mohammad Z[48] describes a graphic Life Review in which he saw himself as a ten-year-old boy mercilessly bullying another lad of comparable age.

> I felt all of the pain and hurt that I had inflicted upon him inside of myself.
>
> When this boy went home to his parents, I saw the impact that seeing him in that state had on his parents. I felt the feeling and pain it created in them and how it affected their behaviour from that point forward. I saw that as a result of this action, his parents would be always more worried when their son was out of home, or if he was a few minutes late.

> I saw that whenever I had done something good to anyone or anything, that I had done it to myself. And whenever I had hurt someone, I had done it to myself.

Following the Life Review, debriefing may take place. This is the first occasion during most afterlife interactions that God invites discussion and is prepared to speak in depth, for as long as needed.

The NDEr by now feels comfortable enough in God's loving presence to ask questions, and they remember doing so. God is reported to answer these in full, although frustratingly many NDErs say the exact information provided is wiped from the memory in part or in total on return to Earth. God often warns the NDEr in advance that this will happen. He is fundamentally not in the business of explaining everything but instead of teaching us to trust him.

What is remembered, though, is the certainty that everything queried had happened for a reason and that God was in ultimate control. He had been creatively and empathetically involved in events in our world and in their individual lives far beyond what they would have suspected.

Maybe we should gain comfort from this, as many of us have questions we would like to ask God that appear to have no acceptable answer in our cultures. We have problems with pain and suffering, and wonder "Why does God allow babies to suffer and die?" Satisfactory answers apparently exist, and were we to ask God such questions in the afterlife, his explanations would surely satisfy us, just as they have done for many NDErs.

A great truth emerges as we ponder God's answering questions but subsequently removing the answers from memory:

> *God deals with humankind **not** as a philosopher might do*
> *but **rather** as a Pastor and a loving, protective Father.*

And although most of us may never have a Near Death Experience with a challenging Life Review, we are all destined to die, and would do well to think through in advance the purposes, interactions and relationships of our own lives. Can and should we be doing better?

God's Purposes

NDEs confirm many important scriptural precepts about God. For example, we have already discovered in Chapter 4, that purpose trumps timing in God's plans.

Thousands of NDErs have reported that they wanted to remain with God in the afterlife—but the commonest response to them has been that their *purpose* had not yet been fulfilled and that they had to return to our world first. Their "mission" on Earth, and the need to complete it, would determine the *timing* of their return to Paradise.

Purpose first—timing second.

Lisa's[49] NDE, due to a head injury at only age 5, illustrates this common experience:

> He tells me, "Lisa, it's not your time to go. Look at your family, they need you. You have a greater purpose in this lifetime and you will succeed in that purpose. You need to go back" ….
>
> I, indeed, went back to my body and my family and my life.

Although the one ubiquitous purpose given NDErs returning to our world is to learn to love and serve others *before it will be an appropriate time for them to return to Paradise*, some are given a more specific insight into their role. This will regularly involve family, even unborn children. Sally Smith[50] was just 9 years old in 1960 when she was told to return:

> Suddenly, a beautiful voice told me that it was not my time, that I had more to do, and that I would marry and have a boy and a girl. I was also told that my life would not be easy, but I would never be alone.

Sally married and has had her boy and girl. She has faced massive challenges—but she reports benefit from overcoming these.

Before proceeding, let's be crystal clear on one point—Almighty God can manifest himself to us in any form he selects, here on Earth or during an NDE. On Earth he generally remains invisible (1 Timothy 1:17):

> Now to the King eternal, immortal, *invisible*, the only God, be honour and glory for ever and ever. Amen.

However, out of love, to facilitate communication and relationship, God may choose to appear to you in the form of a man who radiates light and who communicates telepathically.

Nor is God the Father limited to one place at one time; he, like Jesus and the Holy Spirit, may appear simultaneously to any number of people in different locations.

Please be discerning, because not all spiritual experiences are from God. It is through his words and actions towards us that we will be able to assess whether it is God, purveyor of love, truth and forgiveness, or a deceptive spirit instead who is interacting with us. We need to remain wise and sensitive throughout. This applies to not only our own experiences, but to our embracing the validity of the experiences of others.

God's Home

Why have so many NDErs described a feeling of returning to where they belong when approaching the Light in the afterlife?

Hundreds of NDErs record that they felt "at home" in Paradise, such that the majority did not want to return to life in our world. They had not met with anything there identical to their own earthly homes, so where does this "homely" feeling derive from? I have asked, but NDErs appear not to know the answer themselves.

Nevertheless, returnees habitually hanker to return to being "at home" in Paradise with God. This can prove distressing for them trying to readjust to life on Earth again. The NDE researcher PMH Atwater states on her website that a minimum timespan to successfully integrate the after-effects of an NDE—making what was learned real and workable in everyday life—is seven years. From the range of accounts I have listened to or read, seven years is perhaps an average rather than a "minimum": I have noted that some returnees appear to reintegrate within a few short months, while others appear to me never to have readjusted fully.

Rob N's account, recorded 10th May 2015 number 3938 on the NDERF website, is more detailed than most about "coming home":

> The feelings I experienced were not exactly earthly and they were much more intense than on Earth.
>
> The first feeling was a feeling of intense peace. It was so calm and serene with an incredible amount of tranquility. All of my earthly worries, thoughts, fears, and opinions were gone. The intensity of the tranquility was so incredible, and overwhelming, that there was no fear in what I was experiencing. I had no fear about where I was going and what to expect when I arrived there.
>
> Then I felt warmth. It was as if I were wrapped in a blanket that came out of an oven. It wasn't too hot, nor too cold. The warmth was simply perfect...
>
> Then I felt the love. This is a very difficult feeling to describe. Try to remember the first time you saw your child or met your significant other. Most people know what I am talking about. It is that feeling of first-time love that is so positive and so powerful. Now take that feeling and multiply it thousands of times over. It is a love that is unimaginable on Earth.
>
> Then there was the desire to be *home*, not at my earthly house, but *home* in Heaven. It was overwhelming. The desire to be *home* with all of my loved ones and with GOD (his capitals) was like a massive force pulling me toward it. The force was so strong that I couldn't get away from it even if I wanted to, which I guarantee that I didn't. I wanted to be in the glory of GOD—and to be with all those that have passed on before me.

To this point, Rob's description fits a simple explanation, and one which I surmised could explain the majority of NDErs feeling that they are at home in Paradise. Most if not all NDErs there experience an incredible love and peace—which seems on a par with a baby being soothed lovingly by a mother. I am certain that you and I were designed to respond to love at a truly fundamental level. The love and security felt by a baby in a welcoming parental home may well correlate with the same feelings experienced by an NDEr in Paradise.

However, Rob continues his account and raises another possibility for this surprising sense of "coming home".

> I was on the way home to where I belong *and where I came from*. My soul was now free from earthly bonds. I was traveling *back* from this journey of (gaining) knowledge here on Earth.
>
> The intensity of the feelings was overflowing. It is hard to describe the magnitude of it all, but my faith and belief in God suddenly took over.
>
> I soon came to realise that I was feeling the power of GOD.

Like Rob, a significant number of other NDErs report the impression that they had been with God previously. Perhaps our consciousness (spirit) is formed there, and subsequently "breathed" into our earthly bodies such that we become living beings, as happened to Adam? (Genesis 2:7)

If we do pre-exist our appearance in the world, as suggested by some NDErs and by various scriptures, then entering the afterlife could indeed be a "coming home" of our consciousness, our spirit, our essential selves, despite our bodies having been left behind on Earth.

However, meeting with God in today's Heavenly City, or much more commonly in the gardens of Paradise that surround it, is only a precursor for what he has planned and purposed to come next.

As a Bible-believing Christian, I believe that we occupy our afterlife spirit bodies in the Venues of Hades only until shortly before Judgement Day, when we will be re-clothed in our own physical but now imperishable bodies once more (Romans 8:23).

What happens then, and why?

Whatever God reveals prophetically in advance will provide us with clues to who we *truly* are and why we were created in the first place.

CHAPTER 16

God's Family

> Therefore, if anyone is in Christ, that person is a new Creation. The old has gone, the new has come!
>
> —2 Corinthians 5:17

This book is focusing on God's creativity, past present and future; and who we are and where we fit in.

Whether Creation of life was slow or fast, or involved guided Evolution or not, becomes trivial in the light of God's plans for you personally.

When a person becomes a Christian, God creates in them a new spiritual life and interests. Externally, they may get on with living the way things were—or have more dramatic and obvious changes—but God is always forming new people on the inside.

Why?

God's "Main Game"

I am convinced we have been planned by God before the first atom appeared, to become a member of his personal family—his kids! This is extraordinary and an unexpected privilege.

Creating his own family through adoption is his main intention and very close to his heart. I am reminded of a friend's little 3-year-old adopted girl (now grown) who was overheard explaining to another child, whose mummy was pregnant, that she had not herself grown in her mummy's tummy; instead, she stated very proudly, she had been grown in someone's else's tummy—and given to her mummy and daddy. She saw herself as a special gift, as indeed she is and always will be.

Each person who gives themselves to God the Father through Jesus becomes a special gift and is deeply appreciated by him, and always will be.

Our world and humankind were created for that purpose even before Time started in our Universe.

Genesis 1:27 teaches that humankind were to be designed in the "likeness" of God—the same word is used in Genesis 5:3 of Adam fathering a son, Seth, in his "likeness". This suggests the likeness to be a family one. Paul used a similar argument in Acts 17:29 to discount the belief that God could occupy an idol made by man: "Since we are God's offspring, we should not think that the divine being is like gold or silver or stone". In other words, we are alive and being God's offspring, should appreciate that he too is alive—and thereby cannot be a golden or stone idol any more than we are.

The word translated as "likeness" carries the picture of "one blood" with God, which too carries the sense that we are his children.

The shed blood of Christ on the cross opened the way to us becoming "one blood" with God by adoption. During the commemoration of Christ's sacrifice in communion services, this is one aspect in which I personally rejoice, and thank the Lord for allowing me to be one blood with him.

> John 1:12,13—To all who did receive him (Jesus), to those who believed in his name, he gave the right to become children of God—children born not of natural descent, nor of human decision or a husband's will, but born of God.

> *The primary reason we were created in the first place is that God wants his own family—his adopted children.*
> *This is a massive revelation of who we **really** are, and why.*

God's New Creations

God does not leave new baby believers in the same condition as when he first accepts them into his family. All relationships need to develop step-by-step, and our relationship with God is no different.

God encourages a daily response from us to his initiatives.

We begin to relate in earnest when we believe and accept Jesus as our personal Saviour, but this is only the start of our close relationship. It needs to be nurtured and developed, firstly by communicating. If you met someone just once and never again spent time with them or spoke to them, that friendship would be unlikely to go anywhere.

Similarly, developing a sincere friendship with God requires daily conversational "chatting" with him, even just within ourselves—the Bible describes this as "praying without ceasing" (1 Thesselonians 5:16-18).

There is also focussed praying to our Father, generally with others in mind, as Jesus and the early disciples did.

> *The most important single feature of developing your relationship with God, and understanding his ways, is how you and he spend time together day by day.*

Similar to good earthly fathers, but more effectively, God balances guided development with graded freedom of choice within each of the important dimensions of life.

I remember how when I was first converted, God seemed so close and answered prayer readily—something I have observed in other "newbies". When a new baby cries, adopted or not, you feed it and comfort it.

However, as time goes on, God expects us to take on more and more responsibility for our own development. Faith brings us into his family and must always remain a foundation that deepens and widens, but that is just the start.

He next begins dealing progressively with our character and approach to life, with the ultimate aim of our developing divine love, "agape" in the Greek language (described comprehensively in 1Corinthians 13). The apostle Peter wrote regarding this co-operative development by new adoptees (2Peter 1:4-8):

> He has given us his very great and precious promises, so that through them you may participate in the divine nature, having escaped the corruption in the world caused by evil desires.
>
> For this very reason, make every effort to add to your faith goodness; and to goodness, knowledge; and to knowledge, self-control; and to self-control, perseverance; and to perseverance, godliness; and to godliness, mutual affection; and to mutual affection, love ("agape").
>
> For if you possess these qualities in increasing measure, they will keep you from being ineffective and unproductive in your knowledge of our Lord Jesus Christ.

There are multiple excellent books dealing with this creative input by God into the development of the "new self" (2Corinthians 5:17). It is good for us to read some of them. There is a point I would like to make about these books, though—do not expect your personal experiences to necessarily equate with those of others. God always deals with us as individuals; he made us that way and he knows what is best for us at any particular stage. For some, he may be working with their need to persevere under trials, for others their lack of self-control, and so on. We all begin with "faith", and the ultimate target of "agape" will always remain, but God's direct innovative input and timing into our development and circumstances will vary.

Because "agape" is so vital to us, let's discuss it further, but briefly.

"Agape" was present in Heaven before the world was created. Father and Son related and loved one another in Heaven—for example, Jesus said to God the Father, "You loved me *before* the Creation of the world" (John 17:24). The evidence from other scriptures and from NDErs is that they continue to love and relate in this "agape" way. Presumably so will we, when we join them in the afterlife. The challenge for us is to develop "agape" in our character while on Earth, to prepare ourselves properly for our long-term future.

"Anyone who does not love ("agape") does not know God, because God is love ("agape")." (1John 4:8)

Mother Teresa[51] understood "agape"—she said she was "Seeking the face of God in everything, everyone, everywhere, all the time, and His hand in every happening." Mother Teresa's own ministry, and that of her order The Sisters of Mercy, centred around a practical demonstration of "agape" through loving the unlovely, as Jesus always did.

> "We must love them because it is Jesus in the distressing disguise of the poor. They are our brothers and sisters. They are—all people, those lepers, those dying, those hungry, those naked—they are Jesus. For us it is not sufficient to say, 'Oh, I love Jesus tenderly.' We have to show we love Him by our wholehearted service."

An impacting demonstration of "agape" was given by Jesus when he prayed for his enemies who nailed him to the cross: "Father, forgive them, for they do not know what they are doing" (Luke 23:34). To develop a similar level of love in our lives, we must also learn to "pray for those who persecute you" (Matthew 5:44) and other similar exhortations given by Jesus.

The opportunity to develop this "agape" dimension in our character, that of loving our enemies, is seemingly unique to our lives on our planet; descriptions of the afterlife would support this supposition.

Our lives on Earth take place in a cauldron of good and evil, providing opportunities for personal development unlikely to be repeated.

GOD'S FATHERHOOD

For anyone who chooses to relate to God the Father through Jesus as personal Saviour, the relationship can develop into something very close.

For example, Romans 8:15 and Galatians 4:6 show that Christians may address God the Father as "Abba". This was an Aramaic term that could be used as a title of respect—"Father"—or "Dear Father"—or an even more personal term closer to the relational "Daddy". It is a great privilege to be able to relate to God personally as our "Abba". The scripture in Galatians 4:6,7 suggests this loving familiarity as a member of God's own family is the intended emphasis:

> Because you are his sons, God sent the Spirit of his Son into our hearts, the Spirit who calls out, *"Abba* Father." So, you are no longer a slave, but God's child.

On rare occasions, we find God speaking as a Father to protect a child from danger. I have been told a number of startling examples of this, but will consider just one in detail that involved Liz Lewis, a girl I taught in Africa and who was also a member of the Harvest youth group which Brenda and I helped run.

After school, Liz was camping in a game reserve in Zimbabwe when she heard what she took to be hyenas moving around the bush kitchen. She decided to do what she had done the previous night and get up with a torch to "shoo" them away. I will use her words written especially for me:

> I was about to get up, my hand had already started pulling back the blanket when a quiet voice very clearly and full of authority said, "*Do not move*".
>
> I knew that it wasn't me that said it so it must have been God.
>
> Even though I heard the voice I still pondered on the thought of moving when the voice said again, "*Do not move*".
>
> By this time the animal, that I thought was a hyena, had walked oh so softly to the front of my tent. It sat on its haunches. I could see its shape as the fire was behind it. It was a lion, not a hyena. Boy, did I keep very still. It then got up and moved around the side of the tent to where my head was – I could hear this creature panting slowly. My heart was beating so loudly that I thought the lion would hear it and I felt very fearful.
>
> Thankfully, the lion moved away.
>
> Then the night was filled with screams and shouts. The lion had attacked Roy and Yvonne Jennings in their tent when Roy had banged the canvas to frighten away what he had also assumed to be

a hyena. This movement was what the lion had been watching for, so it ripped through the canvas to get at its prey.

Thankfully the Ranger, Doug Evans, fired shots that frightened the lion off, but both Roy and Yvonne sustained serious injuries.

One thing I find poignant in Liz's case is that she had no continuing contact with her earthly father, so this rescue by her heavenly Father was especially significant for her.

Who are you in actual fact and what is your significance?
Ponder God's fatherhood for answers.

God's "Family Business" on Earth

Once adopted into God's family, we need to be about his "Family Business".

Jesus illustrated this when as a child of twelve he remained behind in the temple to speak with the religious Teachers there while his parents left for home (Luke 2:45-52 in New King James Bible). When Mary found him three days later, she chided him, "Your father and I have sought you anxiously."

He replied, "Why did you seek me? Did you not know that I must be about my Father's Business?"

Mary had been referring to Joseph as his earthly father, but Jesus was claiming a mandate from God as his heavenly Father, to speak for him to the religious leaders.

Christians adopted into God's family inherit the mantle of speaking for the Father, and a vital part of that work includes preaching and teaching Bible truths, alongside other variations of service. As we go along, we must also tell others our personal experiences of answered prayer and other ways God has worked in our lives—and the lives of others we know or know about.

In fact, just as the early Christians gave witness to the breath-taking things God had taught them and done in their own lives and communities, similar vibrant teaching and testimony needs to be renewed with urgency throughout the world. This would be for the sake of unbelievers, but also to encourage and embolden Christians in the face of satanic expansion.

Our "family business" must portray God to the world.

Each Christian should display a fragment of God's nature, love and ministry. The goal is for these fragments to unify and shine such that Father and Son become perceivable and accessible to others in our world, like a mosaic picturing God—visible from the image cast by the combination of different fragments of stone.

The unity God wants is not uniformity, in that he has made us all different such that we all have something unique to contribute to that mosaic. Attempts by different groups to impose unity through uniformity have always ended in failure, and more importantly, have ruined the effectiveness of Christianity in reaching society.

It is heartbreaking, but we see that Christians worldwide are not rising to the degree of spiritual unity that was so much on Jesus' heart shortly before his sacrificial death for us. We can be divided and at times an unattractive and bickering family.

We see that disunity today in realising how many thousands of Christian denominations exist—above 33800 according to the World Christian Encyclopedia in 2001, and thousands more denominations have risen up since then. Consequently, God is not being correctly portrayed to the world—at best, we Christians present a very disorganised, fractured impression of him. Consider the words of the prayer of Jesus to Father God shortly before death (John 17:20,21):

> "My prayer is not for them (the disciples) alone. I pray also for those who will believe in me through their message (including modern Christians), that all of them may be one, Father, just as you are in me and I am in you. May they also be in us, so that the world may believe that you have sent me."

The disunity across Christianity, combined with Satan's relentless discrediting of God, is keeping millions from believing in Jesus. They are consequently not being prepared on an individual level to spend eternity with God as part of his family, which is a shocking tragedy.

Tragically, the greatest displays of unity and the most effective poignant witness to the Lord in our day, as well as throughout the last two thousand years, have come about through the persecution and martyrdom of individual believers, families and whole groups, because of their faith in Christ.

God's Inheritance for His Family

God has the ancient legal right not to provide us with an inheritance at all, or to limit our inheritance, because of our position as adoptees—Jesus is his only personally begotten child. I feel myself that becoming a part of God's family is inheritance enough. He has decided very generously to go much further than that. Consider the verses below:

> So, you are no longer a slave, but God's child; and since you are his child, God has made you also an heir (Galatians 4:7).

> The Spirit himself testifies with our spirit that we are God's children. Now if we are children, then we are heirs—heirs of God and co-heirs with Christ, if indeed we share in his sufferings in order that we may also share in his glory (Romans 8:16-17).

We see how encompassing God the Father's love is for us! We are not only part of his family, but have become *co-heirs* with Christ, providing us with similar rewards to those that Jesus enjoys in the afterlife.

However, this quote in Paul's letter to the Romans suggests that while part of our inheritance is to share in Jesus' glory in the afterlife, this aspect is linked to our sharing in his sufferings. Revilement, mocking and persecution have never been far from the church throughout its history.

Finally, as the icing on the cake, consider Ephesians 1: 4,5

> For he chose us in him *before* the Creation of the world, to be holy and blameless in his sight.
>
> In love, he *predestined* us for adoption to sonship through Jesus Christ, in accordance with his pleasure and will.

God had chosen and predestined us to become family, and thereby also heirs with Jesus, even before the world was created! That makes me feel incredibly privileged and secure in his love.

It is also who we truly are, and why.

God's Family and Satan

What was Satan doing already in the Garden of Eden, right at the start of the appearance of mankind? We live in a fallen world because of the influence of Satan and his cohorts, a world where good and evil co-exist side-by-side.

Satan is described in scriptures as the Prince of this world, and so operates on a worldly stage using some very effective tactics.

> If anyone loves the world, love for the Father is not in them. For everything in the world—the lust of the flesh, the lust of the eyes, and the pride of life—comes not from the Father but from the world. The world and its desires pass away, but whoever does the will of God lives forever (1 John 2:15-17).

Satan's kingdom is temporary and will be dismantled at Judgement. It promises much, but delivers little, and certainly nothing of long-term value. Quite the reverse in fact.

Please be alert and wary, Satan is a supernatural enemy and cannot be defeated by logic or our best efforts. He will test us at every point of our service for God. Even Jesus himself had to overcome Satan's temptations before his public ministry began (Matthew 4:1-11). He was also tested during his ministry, such as when he rebuked Peter (Matthew 16:23).

> *Nevertheless, Satan is not to be feared because a prayerful and obedient relationship with the Lord protects us through the presence and power of the Holy Spirit.*

However, Satan still lurks as our personal enemy while we are in the world. Satan and his minions are this very moment active in many facets of life that include clever lies that are corrupting to our children.

One major target of Satan in our modern world is to denigrate fatherhood and family life; this is the only target I will discuss (briefly) in this book. The more family life can be diminished in the eyes of humankind, the fewer who will be attracted by God the Father's offer of adoption into his own family.

In the world of today, certain children, as an outcome of abuse or family breakdown, may even comprehend Satan more readily and function in his earthly kingdom more naturally than in God's kingdom. I remember talking to a street kid who was involved with demons and demonic power, and who was totally disinterested in Jesus, saying that Jesus could not give him what the demons did. In that analysis he was completely correct. Satan offered him supernatural powers, drugs, sex, thrills—whatever it took to ultimately destroy him.

Satan also desires to work through gangs and certain evil groups and secret societies to attract our youth in their search for acceptance and meaning. Certain sites on social media can do the same, and Satan is even invading our schools through bogus sex education programs carrying names such as "Safe Schools" and its clones, but which are sexually grooming and perverting innocent children from nursery school age upwards.

We need to be alert and expect continuing attacks to discredit the importance of marriage and family life and for these assaults to become more strident until Christ returns. Dividing children from parents and family influence is an effective way Satan can produce followers fanatically and financially loyal to him, and dedicated to his causes. Cult leaders are his allies in this.

Communism was and still is a Satanic political system in its practices. I was reading some old Communist material recently and was shocked once more at how deeply they hated family life, and how determined they were to destroy it. Marxist-leaning groups are having a field day in our universities and other institutions of higher education.

Satan may have changed his colours for our times, but his totalitarian intentions remain—to destroy marriage and the nuclear family, and thereby divert millions away from God's intentions for family and community.

If you think I am exaggerating regarding Satan's intention to attack family life, I will describe an incident that shook me considerably. It occurred in the 1970s when Brenda and I were reasonably new Christians living in Rhodesia. Keen to learn all we could about God, we met in a small group once a week with an experienced Minister who discussed basic Christian teaching with us, as developed by Campus Crusade for Christ. One evening, our Minister was distracted. Eventually, he stopped trying to concentrate on the teaching materials and told us what was disturbing him.

He had just flown back from a Christian conference held in Johannesburg. During the flight, he had wanted to open conversation with the fellow passenger beside him. This man had refused the offer of an in-flight meal. Our Minister opened the conversation.

"Don't you like the flight meals?"

"It's not that. I am praying and fasting."

"Really? I'm a Christian myself and sometimes I pray and fast also."

"I'm not a Christian, I'm a satanist. We are gathering from around the world to fast and pray against Christian marriages, especially the marriages of Christians in leadership."

With this disturbing encounter still on his mind, no wonder our Minister was distracted.

Our group of new Christians was not overly concerned, however. In that era, Christian marriages had statistically a far higher success rate than those in society in general. Almost all the church Ministers we knew appeared to enjoy happy, exemplary marriages, including the young Minister leading our group.

Within a few months of this meeting, we began to hear of Christian marriages in trouble, including those of certain prominent leaders. We were shocked and disappointed.

Eventually, the marriage of that very Minister ended in divorce. (He was deemed the innocent party by other Christian leaders and continued in a very successful youth ministry, remarrying happily later.)

Since then, it is a scandal how many prominent Christian leaders have betrayed their spouses and broken their marriage vows. The divorce rate has rocketed, in certain parts of the Christian church more than others, though some statistics suggest divorce is still a little lower in churches than in society at large. Nonetheless, the rate is certainly much higher than back in the 1970s. Satan knew what he was doing. He still does! He knows that family life is an earthly shadow that prepares us for our relationship with God and he is determined on its failure, alongside our personal undoing as a consequence.

Lest we despair, we must remember that Satan is ultimately a defeated foe, despite much evidence of his influence in our world. Shortly before his own death, Jesus spoke to his disciples realistically about difficulties ahead, but then encouraged them with these words:

> "I have told you these things, so that in me you may have peace. In this world you will have trouble. But take heart! I have overcome the world" (John 16:33).

OUR ULTIMATE FUTURE

While our becoming part of God's family and consequently immortal is clear in scripture, the ultimate purpose for this is kept mysterious. Consider 1John 3:1-2

> See what great love the Father has lavished on us, that we should be called children of God! And that is what we are!
> The reason the world does not know us is that it did not know him.
> Dear friends, now we are children of God, *and what we will be has not yet been made known.*
> But we know that when Christ appears, we shall be like him, for we shall see him as he is.

Therefore, while scripture confirms that our ultimate destiny after Jesus' Second Coming remains shrouded in mystery, yet we are assured of God's fatherly love and support throughout, and that we should be developing within his family right now to be more like Jesus in our character.

Why doesn't God lay it all out in the Bible for us to look at?

I believe it's because one of his prime intentions is for us to learn to "walk by faith and not by sight" (2 Corinthians 5:7). Furthermore, he wants us involved in our earthly development and mission rather than dominated by what is to come.

Nevertheless, being adopted into God's family is without doubt the first essential step into our exciting destiny. Have you taken that step? Unless you do, you will never discover fully who you *really* are and *why*.

Consequently, whether Creation of life was slow or fast, or involved guided Evolution or not, becomes a non-issue in the light of God's overarching plan to produce his own adopted family forever; and for you to be included.

Consider that our old Earth will be destroyed (2Peter3:10-12) making political and climate debates obsolete, while we will continue our new lives on a New Earth.

As when an artist produces a masterpiece, the product takes precedence over the process. Who cares today besides art dealers whether the Mona Lisa was painted in a week or a month? Or what the exact order of the brush strokes were? Debates over Creation and Evolution are like that; they are essentially trivial in comparison with God's masterpiece—which is a family of his own.

> *God's upcoming Venue and our exciting futures will be in*
> *New Heavens on a New Earth, in which we believers will*
> *live as part of a loving, loyal family—God's family.*

An extraordinary and amazing future lies ahead for us. Let's probe our exciting destiny in more detail.

CHAPTER 17

DESTINY

Earth → Hades (Paradise or Prison) → Jesus returns → Our bodily Resurrection → Judgement → New Heavens and New Earth → unrevealed future destiny.

The victory of Christ purchased at Calvary extends for us throughout our earthly life and then beyond.

In the progression above, the Venues and order of events for people who die nowadays is the one I think best fits the scriptures. There are however a range of different opinions on the sequence of God's unfolding plans, and also where and when the thousand-year reign of Christ fits in to that sequence (See Revelation Chapter 20).

Since scripture is clear regarding purposes but nearly always unclear regarding the timings and order of future events, cases can be made for other possible sequences, and many scholars have done so.

However, we saw earlier that it is almost impossible to predict how and when God will fulfil biblical prophecy, and history reveals that it usually comes as a big surprise just how the prophecies were brought to pass. I expect the same will be true with prophecies about the future; we will be marvelling amongst ourselves, looking back, just how amazingly God has achieved them.

In fact, Jesus warned his disciples at his Ascension into Heaven about wanting to know the specific timing of divine actions, when they asked when he would restore God's Kingdom in Israel. Instead, he told them firmly: "It is not for you to know the times or dates the Father has set by his own authority…" (Acts 1:7). I wish all modern disciples paid attention to Jesus' words before launching into their own interpretations of events leading to the end of the world; much unnecessary confusion has resulted plus false predictions that have belittled the Christian church worldwide.

Consequently, I will in this chapter remain centred on the upcoming *events* themselves, rather than speculating on the order and "times or dates" in which they will occur. What happens to us and our response is far more significant to Father God and to ourselves than our efforts at speculating about how the future will unfold.

Many Christians believe that our spirits nowadays go straight to the City in Heaven when we die, to wonderful rooms or mansions prepared there for us by Christ. This may or may not be so for martyrs (Rev 6: 9-11) and certain specially chosen individuals like Enoch and Elijah, who the Bible tells us were transported bodily to be with God.

However, most people currently leave their physical bodies behind at death and will be re-embodied only at humankind's resurrection shortly before Judgement. Until then, they continue in their spirit bodies in Hades (Paradise or Prison sections). Jesus is also to be found there in Hades, although he has other roles in the heavenly city itself, such as interceding for us before the throne of the Father, and preparing for his return to Earth.

It should be a relief to know we will eventually have perfect and incorruptible bodies, because to be fully ourselves we need our bodies; think how frequently you use your hands in the things you do as one minor example. Even when a single thumb is out of commission due to injury, we come to realise how helpful it has been to us. No wonder so many NDErs have reported extreme frustration when trying to touch or hold things while still in their spirit bodies on Earth, only to have their hands pass straight through those things, or even through the people they were trying to touch. Here is a typical account given by Dr Dianne Morrissey[52]:

> As I looked through the walls of my house toward the front sidewalk, I noticed a man walking down the street. Eagerly, I "flew" to him, right through the walls, and tried to get his attention. Staring deeply into his eyes, I said forcefully, "Can you help me? I need help." Then I tried to shake his shoulders, but he still didn't notice me. Frustrated, I tried to touch his shoulder to get him to look at me, and my hand went through his upper right shoulder blade and out his back. This startled me.
>
> "What am I to do?" I wondered, becoming upset when I realised that the man could neither see nor hear me.

These common experiences suggest that the spirit body and spirit material is not composed of atoms at all. Why should it be? God can use any building bricks he chooses for his Creations, with any properties he designates.

However, our resurrected bodies will be material ones again and similar to Christ's at his resurrection. He could be seen, touched, eat fish, walk and talk and so on—although he did display a few new properties such as appearing suddenly in a locked room, and also disappearing from sight. Overall, though, our lives such as we are used to on Earth in physical bodies should resume.

Some Christians have told me they believe that Jesus has already led believers out of Hades and into Heaven in a kind of victory pageant, and that all Christians who have died since have gone directly to Heaven.

The early church did not believe nor teach this. The early church taught about Hades/Sheol as the destination before Judgement Day of all spirits after death, including the spirits of Christians. Detailed confirmatory writings have survived from the third century—for example by Tertullian (AD 160-225 approx) and Hippolytus (AD 170-236 approx), as well as further writings but of disputed authorship; all describe the spirits of humankind, righteous and unrighteous, waiting in Hades until the Second Coming to Earth of Christ. They believed, however, that martyrs were honoured by being an exception who were already in Heaven.

The experiences of reliable Christians who have "died" and returned, including a number of respected Ministers such as Bob Bosworth, Timothy LaFond, Don Piper, Howard Pittman, Roy Royston, Howard Storm, Dirk Willner, BJ McKelvie, George Rodonaia, and Ian McCormack—suggest that the theology of the early church is correct. During their NDEs, each of these modern Ministers, besides others, have experienced Hades in spirit bodies and were not in the Heavenly City.

Most Ministers who have had afterlife experiences in recent times had some very different denominational expectations from what was happening to them. This is because their church theology, or lack of it, differed from the correct theology of the early church.

The early church also taught that after Judgement, God will provide a fresh beginning for his redeemed family in a New Jerusalem on a New Earth in New Heavens (perhaps a fresh Cosmos). Churches that teach that are in line with scripture.

The heavenly city and surroundings where God the Father and Jesus live today will be remodelled in the New Jerusalem. Why will God change his habitat?

> *God the Father wants to live amongst his*
> *kids, the family that he is adopting.*

Revelation 21:2-5 describes the glimpse of this shown to the Apostle John:

> I saw the Holy City, the New Jerusalem, coming down out of Heaven from God, prepared as a bride beautifully dressed for her husband.
> And I heard a loud voice from the throne saying, "Look. God's dwelling place is now among the people, and *he will dwell with them. They will be his people, and God himself will be with them and be*

their God. He will wipe every tear from their eyes. There will be no more death or mourning or crying or pain, for the old order of things has passed away."

He who was seated on the throne said, "I am making everything *new.*"

As we might have predicted using the Transfer Principle, descriptions by NDErs of the Heavenly City where God dwells right now share similarities with the New Jerusalem to come after Judgement. However, there are some differences; the one to come would appear to be even more majestic.

Humans on our planet can change where they live and move from one address to another as it suits them. Soon after Judgement, God the Father will move to the New Jerusalem, from where he will reign with Jesus.

One nice touch is that we can all start afresh together in the stunning new Venue. It will have been cleansed from Satan's evil presence and cohorts, and from all previous sin.

Thankfully, accepting Christ's offer of salvation for ourselves is the antidote to a punitive Judgement and releases us from any fear of punishment after death, and ensures our names will be found in the Book of Life at Judgement. John 3:16 and other verses confirm this great opportunity. Although it is true that "the wages of sin is death" (Romans 6:23), that same debt has been paid in full by Jesus dying in our place, a substitutionary death, which explains why the "wages of sin" verse continues:

> For the wages of sin is death, *but the gift of God is eternal life in Christ Jesus our Lord.*

As is the case with any gift offered to you, you are free to accept or reject it, even as you read this. Your choice will be respected by God and will prevail.

After Judgment, there will be no more need to maintain an empty Hades because its Prison and Paradise sections will then be deserted. Death will likewise cease because life will be eternal, either on God's New Earth, or in Hell. Revelation 20:13,14 describes this clearly:

> Death and Hades gave up the dead that were in them, and each person was judged according to what they had done.
> Then Death and Hades were thrown into the lake of fire.

Once again, we see the past tense is used. From God's creative viewpoint in Heaven, it is already an accomplished fact, hence the past tense. For humankind today, it will be a future event.

One overall purpose for the return of Christ to the world is not a mystery—it is *restoration*. Consider Acts 3:21, "Heaven must receive him (Jesus) *until* the Time comes for God to restore everything, as he promised long ago through his holy prophets".

*Therefore, Christ's return to Earth from Heaven will be characterised by the **restoration** of all things.*

Even the partial restoration in spiritual bodies witnessed by NDErs in Paradise in modern times is thrilling—youth, mental prowess and physical health appear to be reinstated: the blind can see, the deaf can hear, and amputated limbs are returned.

Nevertheless, a fair Judgement in the future is also implicit, and signalled—in Life Reviews, in unpleasant NDEs such as reported by some failed suicides, in afterlife "prison" communities in Hades (1Peter 3:19,20), and reports by returnees that they have been warned of an impending end to the present world system. If the Second Coming is *genuinely* going to restore "all things", then God's justice must also be restored amongst us, and evil must be judged and sentenced.

If you are in a frothy "feel good" church where sin and judgement are never mentioned, it is opportune to consider an alternative.

Restoration will be the obvious hallmark of Christ's return, and will delight us. We know that we live in a world less perfect than originally created by God, and some of this has been the consequence of human sin, as related in Genesis 3:17-19. It is a world for all its beauty that contains evil, sin and personal destruction.

But at the end of this age, Jesus will rule and reign from his throne in a wonderfully restored New Jerusalem on the New Earth, and we who love him will share in his immortality. Children will have lost all fear of the future, in large part because of Christ's teaching and promises.

Isaiah 54:12-14 anticipates the more detailed descriptions in Revelation of this New Jerusalem:

> I will make your battlements of rubies,
> your gates of sparkling jewels,
> and all your walls of precious stones.
> All your children will be taught by the LORD,
> and great will be their peace.
> In righteousness, you will be established.

The accounts of a number of children who have experienced the afterlife is that their education is continued. Some, such as Colton Burpo[53], claim that Jesus personally taught them. Further learning is planned for us too after Judgement.

Godly government will be a significant feature of the restoration process.

There will be in the New Jerusalem the Tree of Life, laden fruit trees and a flowing river. The Garden of Eden in Genesis sounded idyllic enough, but now the Tree of Life is not going to be forbidden, there is no Tree of

Knowledge of Good and Evil, the fruit trees bear abundantly, and they also have healing properties in their leaves! Eden was the source of a river that branched and flowed out into the surroundings, but the river that begins in the New Jerusalem is different in that it flows out from the very throne of God (Revelation 22:1,2).

All these restorations and developments will benefit us!

Everything Jesus restores at the Second Coming will generate a fantastic, ongoing experience for believers.

During this great restoration, the New Heavens and the New Earth will represent a brand-new start for those who love God. The most exciting thing of all is not the restoration, however, but that Father God and Jesus will be reigning there.

Revelation 22:3-5 tells us:

> The throne of God and of the Lamb will be in the city, and his servants will serve him. They will see his face, and his name will be on their foreheads.
>
> There will be no more night. They will not need the light of a lamp or the light of the sun, for the Lord God will give them light.
>
> And they will reign for ever and ever.

A sun, as created for the first Earth on Day 4 of Creation, will not be required for the New Earth. Father and Son will be the illumination in the New Jerusalem (Revelation 21:23), manifesting their glorious energy. Perhaps they will not limit it, as they do during encounters with people on our planet. Certainly, our glorious, resurrected bodies will be remodelled for the new conditions on the New Earth, and will include eyes that are not damaged by the powerful divine light seen there.

Consider a further feature found in Isaiah 65:17—"The former things will not be remembered, nor will they come to mind", which will include mourning, pain and sorrow, "for the old order of things has passed away" (Revelation 21:4).

In other words, the restoration will be complete, and a new order of reality will be ushered in. New—but having sufficient tags to the past that we will adapt to it quickly.

To summarise, the "shadows" of Heaven experienced on Earth will give way to a new clarity and dimension of glory during these restoration events.

What awaits us is incomprehensible in its love and majesty. 1Corinthians 2:9 exclaims:

> What no eye has seen,
> what no ear has heard,
> *and what no human mind has conceived—*
> are the things God has prepared for those who love him.

Believers can be certain that, in Time, because of Christ's sacrifice for us, we will pass from our present world of the dying into the thrilling eternal presence of God, clothed in glorious, immortal resurrection bodies. We can look forward to being active, loved and loving members of his family. We can confidently anticipate an awe-inspiring destiny, whether we are still here when Christ returns, or whether we have departed to Paradise earlier. Let's live in anticipation, like the early Christians:

> "The Lord will rescue me from every evil attack and will bring me safely to his heavenly kingdom. To him be glory for ever and ever. Amen." (2Timothy 4:18)

> "For our citizenship is in Heaven." (Philippians 3:20)

> "Praise be to the God and Father of our Lord Jesus Christ. In his great mercy, he has given us new birth into a living hope through the resurrection of Jesus Christ from the dead, and into an inheritance

that can never perish, spoil or fade. This inheritance is kept in Heaven for you". (1Peter 1:3,4)

Who are we *really*? What is our origin and destiny?

We are God's Creation in his likeness and image and can be adopted into his family alongside Jesus.

Our destiny then becomes amazing, exciting and secure.

ACKNOWLEDGEMENTS

Many, many thanks to Brenda, my patient wife and editor, who does a marvellous job of turning my rough higgledy-piggledy manuscripts into far better English and much sounder and more pleasing structures. This takes her weeks of frowning and somehow fitting it in despite the other demands on her life. She is a darling!

My "readers" have been vitally important to the finished product. These are unsuspecting friends conned into helping me by reading and criticising the initial rough text – and by "rough" I mean unedited and uncorrected. They ask questions regarding what I meant in certain statements, challenge certain concepts I propose, and identify sections that are boring and need livening up. I could not do without them! For this book, they were Peter and Julie Tennett, Rick and Margaret Ford, Jennifer Bishop, who also helps as my publicist, Geoff Hughes, and my son-in-law David Yates.

My friend from Harvest days, Pete Taylor, has twice arrived in Australia from Ohio at opportune times to help with referencing this book and the previous one and sister book—*Living Beyond: Making Sense of Near Death Experiences*.

My schoolfriend and fellow author, Pastor Roland Pletts, has cast a professional eye over my "finished" text and made a whole lot more corrections, as has Julie Tennett! How could I and Brenda have missed all those necessary adjustments that they picked up? I have found in previous books too that the more sets of eyes that peruse the unfinished manuscript the better.

Special thanks to those who have provided the invaluable endorsements found at the start. When you break new ground, as I have done in this book, you are insecure until people you respect find it interesting and valid.

All have played a significant role towards my goal of wanting readers to get something out of this book. Thank you, you are very very much appreciated.

I would love to know what my readers think of this book! Please consider giving comments about it on social media or email ivanrudolph46@gmail.com with your comments.

ENDNOTES

Preface

1. Albert Einstein (1941)–The Conference on Science, Philosophy and Religion, in Their Relation to the Democratic Way of Life, Inc., New York.

Introduction

2. Gallup Poll plus Conservative Research Averages. Conservative Research Averages
3. The Israel Museum, Jerusalem (2017)–*The Great Isaiah Scroll.*

1—Questioning Evolution

4. Peter J Kreeft (2016) – *Yes or No? Straight Answers to Tough Questions.*
5. Charles Darwin (1859)–*Origin of Species Chap. VI.*

2—The Inspired Answer

6. Attributed to Orwell by associates, but not yet found in his own writings. First published quote appears to be in–*"Partners in Ecocide: Australia's Complicity in the Uranium Cartel"* (1982) by Giorgio Venturini.

3—Pondering a Miracle of Healing

7. C.S. Lewis (1972) – "Miracles" from *God In The Dock*

4—Glimmerings of Time

8. Lyndon F Harris (1997) – *Divine Action: An Interview with John Polkinghorne, Ex-Professor of Mathematical Physics at Cambridge.*
9. Professor Peter Stoner (1976) – *Science Speaks.*

5—Digging Deeper into Time and Prophecy

10. Billy Graham (2013)–*Billy Graham in Quotes*

6—Time in Heaven

11. Todd Burpo (2010)–*Heaven Is For Real.*

7—NDEs, Shadow Theory, and Transfer Principle

12. Near Death Experiences Research Foundation (NDERF) website, exceptional stories, Barbara D 4421, recorded 10/30/2017.
13. Fiona M, Near Death Experiences Research Foundation (NDERF) website, 4346, recorded 5/30/2017.
14. Kerry Packer (1990) – *The Daily Star, Wed. December 28, 2005*
15. Robert Lanza (2014) – *Does Death Exist?*
16. Maurice Rawlings (1978) – *Beyond Death's Door.*

8—Two Stage Theory and God's Creativity

17. Arnold J. Toynbee (1987) – *A Study of History.*
18. Near Death Experiences Research Foundation (NDERF) website, NDE Stories, Jeanne MK 3994, recorded 8/15/2015.

9—The Words of Creation

19. Peter Haycock (2004) – *For Heaven's Sake!!*

10—Genesis Unlocked: Key Words Of Creation

20. Ian McCormack (2008) – *A Glimpse of Eternity.*

11—The Days Of Creation (Genesis 1:1 to 2:3)

21. Richard Sigmund (2004) – *My Time in Heaven.*
22. Professor Peter Stoner (1976) – *Science Speaks.*
23. Sir Lee Brenton (1844)–*English Translation of the Greek Septuagint Bible.*
24. Dr David Instone-Brewer (2015) – *Christianity* magazine August 2015.
25. Stephen Hawking (2015) – *Christianity* magazine August 2015.
26. Kurt Eggenstein (1984)–*Materialistic Science on the Wrong Track.*
27. Bruce B. Miller (2011) – *Your Life in Rhythm p12.*
28. Alpha History of France (2017) – *Remaking France.*
29. Elaine Vornholt and Laura Lee Vornholt-Jones (2008) – *The Soviet Experiment: Playing with Weeks.*

12—Origins (Genesis 2.4 onwards)

30. Pope Francis (2013) – *NY Times Sep 18 2013: An Interview with Pope Francis.*

13—God Speaks Creatively

31. Rev. Frank Mussell (1982) – *Miracle Valley.*

14—Qualities of God

32. Anne Lamott (1994) – Noyes is quoted in Anchor Books, *Bird by Bird.*
33. Dexter Froude, from an account recorded especially for me.
34. Angie Fenimore (1995)–*Beyond the Darkness.* Angie Fenimore (1995)
35. Near Death Experiences Research Foundation (NDERF) website, NDE Stories, Erica P 3997, recorded 8/15/2015.

15—God In Our Afterlife Experiences

36. Near Death Experiences Research Foundation (NDERF) website, NDE Stories, Mindy B 3898, recorded 3/8/2015.
37. Near Death Experiences Research Foundation (NDERF) website, NDE Stories, Laura M 2995, recorded 3/31/2012.
38. Crystal McVea (2013)–*Waking Up in Heaven*.
39. Captain Dale Black (2010)–*Flight to Heaven*.
40. *PMH Atwater (1995) – Beyond the Light*.
41. *PMH Atwater (1995) – Beyond the Light*.
42. Kimberly Clark-Sharp (1995) – *After the Light*.
43. Near Death Experiences Research Foundation (NDERF) website, NDE Stories, Laura M 2995, recorded 3/31/2012.
44. Near Death Experiences Research Foundation (NDERF) website, NDE Stories, Pegi R 2930, recorded 12/31/2011.
45. Kevin Williams (2002) – *Nothing Better Than Death*.
46. Kevin Williams (2002) – *Nothing Better Than Death*.
47. Near Death Experiences Research Foundation (NDERF) website, NDE Stories, Alexa 76, recorded 9/30/2001.
48. Near Death Experiences Research Foundation (NDERF) website, NDE Stories, Mohammad Z 3991, recorded 8/14/2015.
49. Near Death Experiences Research Foundation (NDERF) website, NDE Stories, Lisa 4039, recorded 10/24/2015.
50. Near Death Experiences Research Foundation (NDERF) website, NDE Stories, Sally Smith 3804, recorded 11/15/2014.

16—God's Family

51. Mother Teresa (1995) - *Heart of the World: Thoughts, Stories and Prayers*.

17—Destiny

52. Dr Dianne Morrissey[5] (2002) – *Anyone Can See The Light*.
53. Todd Burpo (2010) – *Heaven Is For Real*.

www.ingramcontent.com/pod-product-compliance
Lightning Source LLC
Chambersburg PA
CBHW071234080526
44587CB00013BA/1606